CONFESSIONS OF A HIGH STRUNG WOMAN

ABBI WALKER

Copyright © 2020 Abbi Walker

ISBN: 978-1-7365511-0-3

For every little girl who has ever been told she was too much.

ABOUT THE AUTHOR:
ABBI WALKER

Abbi Walker is a High Strung Woman obsessed with freedom. Born into the 4th generation of a Southern Baptist preaching family, Abbi has known all too well the pressure to "behave" on a spirited woman with big dreams. She has been fighting like hell to make her own way since before she could walk the aisles of the church house. You can hear her feisty spirit and deep soul in her music, where she has written, produced, recorded and toured 4 albums, through her podcast, and now in her first book. It doesn't matter if she is singing, writing, performing, or speaking- Abbi goes big. Somehow, she always manages to leave you feeling stronger, sassier and more empowered to be the full-on, real YOU. In her first published work, Abbi's honesty, vulnerability and humor lay the foundation for a sacred place of real conversations between the author and her readers. She's no distant instructor- teaching lofty philosophies of impossible ideals. Abbi's own face is covered with the sweat and dust of the dirt of the arena as she whispers secret maneuvers she's learned along the way to the women on either side of her as they face off once again with the enemies that are desperate to subdue them. She is a warrior for women, a big-haired, grinning vigilante helping lead others to a God who breaks chains, shatters expectations, and disintegrates beliefs that hold women back from their full strength, significance, and glory. Her secrets of freedom can always be traced back to Jesus, to an audaciously authentic relationship with God that forever changed her. Abbi introduces her readers to a God who is crazy about them, and shares the wisdom He has taught her that will revolutionize the way they live as strong women in this world. Abbi's message is one of resounding freedom, fierce hope, and radical celebration.

Abbi and her husband Ryan Petkoff live in Dallas, Texas with their perfect, yet terrible-at-times vizsla pup: Bexar. They can be found playing shows together (Ryan plays a mean guitar and co-writes), cheering for their Kansas City Chiefs, hiking in Montana, or drinking margaritas on a patio in the sunshine and laughing until they can't breathe.

INSTAGRAM:
@abbiwalkerofficial and @highstrungwoman
#highstrungwoman #COAHSW
#proudtobeahighstrungwoman #abbiwalker

FACEBOOK:
Confessions Of A High Strung Woman
Abbi Walker Official

WEBSITE:
www.abbiwalker.net
www.abbiwalkermusic.com

MUSIC:
You can find Abbi's albums Feisty, Kiss Kiss Bang Bang, and Hope Of A Little Green on iTunes, Spotify, and Amazon Music.

PODCAST:
The "Confessions Of A High Strung Woman" podcast can be found anywhere podcasts are available, as well as on the website.

THE HIGH STRUNG WOMAN

This one is for the strong, fierce hearted, beautifully complex and profoundly brilliant High Strung Women who have been misunderstood and mistreated for far too long.

We've heard from every direction that we are….
Too emotional.
Too strong.
Too sensitive.
Too passionate.

Too much.
And yet somehow not enough.

When all we see and hear from the world around us is
that who we are, and how we are - is wrong,
and at the same time that what we are <u>not</u>- is "right":
we can turn on ourselves in a very deep and profound way.

Oh but Sis, do I have a story to tell you.
A tale of uprising, freedom, acceptance, joy and empowerment that is no fairytale. There is a life so good that you can't stand it on the other side of this story, and I am so humbled and deeply honored to get to share it with you.

Welcome, my dear sisters, to these
Confessions Of A High Strung Woman.

CONTENTS

PART 1 THE JOURNEY

PART II SELF CARE

ACKNOWLEDGMENTS

When I dreamed of being married as a young girl, and even beyond, I dreamed of a partner to get to chase dreams with. I dreamed of a brave, strong, handsome man that I would proudly walk and work alongside. I never could have dreamed up the man God gave me, who surpasses those ideals and more. Peter Ryan Petkoff, your fearless love and total acceptance of me has changed me forever. You gave me your courage when I didn't have any left, you led me back when I lost my way, and you courageously helped to edit this book. You may have also said, "This might be my actual worst nightmare: to try to edit a book my wife has written about being a *high-strung woman*." And yet, in the middle of Chiefs football season and a global pandemic, you grabbed my hand and led me up the steep trail. I'll never forget it. You did also call my liberal use of commas, "nothing short of offensive to the Queen's language", but you have only won my heart more by joining me in this battle. You make me laugh. You make me believe. I adore you, and I love you with every part of my being. This book would not exist without you, and we all consider you the bravest among us for daring to edit your wife's book.
(It should also be noted, although not unexpected, that I did not heed all of his edits, so any flaws you may find are the result of a stubborn woman, not the skills of my editor.)

God hand-picked the father He knew my wild heart, rebel soul and big personality would need, and boy did He ever deliver. David Walker is my hero. He has shown me the vibrance of a life that dares to challenge the system and chase the real Jesus. He has taught me to love the wild, unbroken trail of going your own way. Sitting under his anointing and preaching has inspired me to preach that which *I* know, and he has been after me to write this book for years. There is something about a Dad who knows you can do it, even when you don't, that just makes you want to try. Thank you for believing in me Dad. I love you and could not be more proud to be your daughter.

My Momma, Shirley Walker. Your spunk, creativity and fierce tenacity have shown me a world of possibility as a woman with a calling on her life, and a message in her heart. You have never been the most conventional of mothers, but your wild adventure-loving heart has made this daughter brave. Thank you for battling for me, taking over the Merch table to sell shirts at shows across Texas, and for praying for me as I have written this book. I love you fiercely.

Allison Lyles. I am convinced there is no greater encourager, prayer warrior or spiritual cheerleader than you. This book never could have been lived, much less written without you. I can never express how grateful I am that God made you be my best friend! You've been hyping me up to chase my dreams for 12 years now and you're my fave. I love you BIG.

Kate Ritter. God gives some people sisters, but He gave me a best friend that also happened to be my little sister. The depth of your love and generosity for others, especially me, consistently leaves me stunned. You are a rare and precious gift to me and to this world, and the way you have loved, prayed for, and supported me through this season has meant the world to your sassy big sister. She thinks you are the most gorgeous, brilliant, warrior hearted woman in the world.

Papa Bear (Jerry Smith). Thank you for knowing the real me, for loving the real me, and for calling me out of hiding again and again to show up in my life as the real me. This book would not exist without you and Miss Lida. You make me brave. I love you both more than you will ever know.

Lida Smith. 15 years ago you agreed to mentor a frustrated, pent-up, wild-hearted and striving young woman. You changed my life. You were the first spitfire of a woman I had ever seen that was wrapped in and convinced of God's goodness and His love, and at the same time walked in power and the full expression of who she was. You weren't in conflict with yourself, you were empowered. I didn't know that was my dream for myself until I saw it in you. I love you so. Thank you for loving me, teaching me, and praying for me.

Brandi Johnson. What a gift to have such an incredible, lifelong friend. Anyone who has known you through Middle School knows the real you, and girl, you have seen some things! Hah! Thank you for loving me so well all these years, and encouraging me to finish this damn book. You are my kindred spirit. I love you.

Wendy. If you ever wonder if you are doing what God made you to do, I am living proof that you are. God has used you in the most profound ways to lead me towards His true heart and freedom. Thank you for taking on such a bad therapy client. I'm sure I'm not supposed to say this, but I love you dearly and am eternally grateful for you.

To the women who have encouraged me along the way, checked in on me, and contended for me in prayer: Erinn Walker, Becca Hall, Kathy Donovan, Elaine, Jamie and Kailyn Petkoff. I love you all so much!!!

Cara Alwill. I am beyond grateful for your mentorship and the breathtaking freedom with which you share your hard fought wisdom as a highly successful, independent, self-published author. Thank you for not only blazing the trail for women like me, but for showing me how to travel it and chase down my own dreams! Praying the biggest blessings over you!

To my incredible, fabulous grandmothers Elaine Morrow and Jane Walker: thank you for paving the way for me in so many ways. I love you both dearly!

INTRODUCTION

In a million different ways, I really believe God called me to write this book just so I could read it and preach it back to myself. To remind myself of the truth He has brought into my life to set me free, to bring such joy, and to forever change the way I knew Him. This book was not been written by a woman who has figured it all out, this book has been bled, sweat, and cried through by a woman who on a daily basis is at some point face down in the arena with a mouth full of dirt, trying to figure out how to stand back up and keep going! But oh, the joy of showing up in the world as the real you, in all of your power and beauty as a High Strung Woman is worth the mouth full of dirt every.single.time!!!!

I'm not an expert on anything other than my own story, my journey, and my truths. This little book was born out of a blog entry that I wrote over 6 years ago, sometime in between driving across Texas to play shows as I chased my dream in music. I really didn't think anyone would ever read it, I just needed to work out my thoughts on feeling both frustrated with my intense personality, as well as proud of the progress I was starting to make in finally understanding myself. It required more words than a 3 minute song would allow, so I cracked open my laptop and let all the words come tumbling out. I hit publish, hopped back out on the road to another show, and completely forgot about it.

But I started getting emails time-stamped at 2 am from women who had found it while googling "high strung" after another argument with their significant other about being too difficult. Email after email came in from women who had big feelings and didn't know what to do with them, strong women who were struggling to find their way in a world full of well behaved ladies, and from women who were raising high strung daughters and were at their wits end because they just couldn't understand them.

Over the next 5 years- those kinds of emails just kept coming. The blog post hardly went viral, but it became clear that there were many other High Strung Women out there and it was time to step up to share my story, the things I had learned that changed my life, and to partner with God to call them forth in all of their glory.

But I fought writing this book like the devil. I didn't want to pick a fight with a world that's nothing short of vicious on any given day. Being a woman with something to say right now may look exhilarating, but I assure you- it feels much more terrifying most days. I have come to see that it feels terrifying because it's so desperately needed. Our world is aching for authenticity and truth- the kind of truth that is bigger than opinion or speculation, and that lit a fire in me to be brave.

I am a 4th generation preacher's daughter and I know all of the "right" things to say and how to say them, and yet, Jesus has set me free from the pretense and invited me into the personal. The kind of relationship where I don't have to change how I really talk when I come to talk to Him. I can come to Him as I am, and we have some *real* conversations. The way I communicate with Him and with you may stir your heart and relieve your soul from all the tight restrictions of religion, it may challenge you, or it may offend you. Either way, I'm good.

I have chosen to refuse to show up as anything other than the real me in these pages. You are going to get a whole lot of sass, humor, honesty, and a holy fire to fight for you that will likely sound like my wild-eyed preaching ancestors. Finding freedom fires me up in way that nothing else does.

I intentionally wrote in the "voice" that I speak in on a daily basis: passionate, sassy, and honest. You are not holding a literary work of art in your hands, but you are holding a fiercely authentic collection of thoughts, insights, and practices that have changed my life as a High Strung Woman. That's another thing- I chose to capitalize and not hyphenate "High

Strung Woman" because we are a force to behold, and the phrase has taken on a strong identity that I felt deserved it's own title, and grammatical rules (much to the dismay of my editor).

I will also often use the term "Sis" when speaking to you, my beloved reader, with all of the love, respect, sass and friendship that comes from such a word down here in the South. The endearing nickname comes from much of my dialogue with my best friend, Devine-Texas-raised and Medina-County-Fair-Queen-Alumni, Allison Lyles. It's the signal for "real talk" in our conversations, as well as the introduction to statements of humor, insight, and wildly outlandish claims that can only come out of the kind of camaraderie brave, honest conversations between close friends can hold. When you hear it, I hope you feel loved, close, and on the inside. This is a safe space, a holy space and I am so honored you'd join me here.

So, Sis it's about to get real. We are going to laugh, speak our truths, and find our way to the kind of freedom that will change your whole damn life. We are done trying to make ourselves smaller, less emotional, or better behaved. We are done living in conflict with ourselves, and done believing that God is mad at us.

Your whole world is about to open up Sis. Let's ride.

PART I
The Journey Of A High Strung Woman

CHAPTER 1
"FOR THE LOVE OF GOD WOMAN, TONE IT DOWN."
- Everyone I Ever Met

My name is Abbi Walker, and I have all of the feelings, all of the opinions and all of the words - *all* the damn time.

I am the walking definition of a "High Strung Woman," and for most of my life, I believed it was some kind of curse. My big emotions and excessive strength of spirit only seemed to alienate me from the things I longed for, and from those I loved. And yet, the tiger in my chest would not be denied.

You see, for as long as I can remember being alive, I have always known one thing: **I *feel* everything**. And, I feel everything ***deeply***. I mean, I feel things all the way down in my bones, and it doesn't matter if it is a big thing or a little thing. My feelings are deep and strong all of the time, and trying to hide them has been nothing short of disastrous.

Now, the reason that you hold this book in your hands today is that this fire in my soul had honestly caused me more grief than good for most of my life. It's as if no matter where I went, my supersized boombox blared Beyonce's *Run The World/GIRLS*, while everyone else in the room was quietly and respectfully playing young Taylor Swift on their Walkmans.

Funny thing is, my stereo was stuck on full blast. Always has been. And I've found that there's just no moving it. My speakers cranked sass, strength, independence and a whole lot of bass, and I was nothing short of disruptive to a world of well-behaved ladies who dared not make a sound.

Try as I might, there was just no way around it. I have been emotional, strong, passionate and "high-strung" every single day that I have walked upon God's green Earth, AND it has only seemed to grow in intensity with each passing year.

, I can't turn off, y'all. I sure as hell haven't found a dimming switch, and for most of my life, the resounding reaction from everyone around me has been,

"For the love of God woman, would you just tone it down?"

Now, in all fairness, this isn't some new personality phenomenon brought on by an almost-millennial generation raised with participation trophies or interpretive dance. This force has been rumbling inside of me every day of my life for as long as I can remember. I now know that I come from a long line of High Strung Women on BOTH sides of my family, so your girl comes by it honestly.

At just 3 years old, I was already a pint-sized pistol with big eyes, a heavy Texas accent, a huge imagination and very strong opinions. I was a tiny firecracker of words, spirit and sass. Oh the sass.....

Dear Lord, bless my parents. Bless them. I was a lot to handle, and everyone knew it.

But no one taught me to be this way. This has just been who I am from the moment I opened my eyes in my poor Momma's arms.

Even before I could form complete sentences, I was a very small, very loud person with big eyes and only one operating speed: *pedal to the metal.*

No matter what I was feeling, I felt it down in my soul. It rattled my bones, and I expressed myself accordingly.

Everything was a big deal to me, and unfortunately for my sweet, more mild mannered Mama, I felt and expressed myself just as strongly about about wanting Cheerios, what time I had to go to bed, scraping my knee, or even my grief after some much deserved discipline for "sassing my Dad" (this would be a repeat offense in my life). All of those things seemed to matter the SAME to me in terms of passion and feeling. Having to go to bed early and miss out on fun hurt my little heart just as badly as slamming my finger in the door, and I expressed myself accordingly.

Think I'm wrong, or perhaps, just a nutcase?

Let's start with a baseline of how reasonable and unfiltered children are. Try reasoning with a toddler about why it's irrational to have their heart broken when the animal crackers are all gone.

No really, I want to hear how that goes, because I've tried it, and if there's anything I've learned in my "I'm-just-an-aunt babysitting" stage of life, it's that toddlers can be completely irrational, emotional terrorists. They will break your heart with their sobs and then ice.you.out. You have done them wrong. It doesn't matter why there are no more crackers, they don't care. But they *will* hold you personally responsible. I have found that with even the cutest, sweetest tempered child, there is just no reasoning with an angry toddler. They do NOT negotiate with grownups, but they will absolutely take prisoners.

Now to be fair, I remember feeling things so deeply in my OWN emotional-terrorist-tiny-toddler-heart, that it would escape from the inside of me to the outside of my little body through shrieks of joy, shivers of excitement, or sobs of disappointment - never to be consoled again.

Viola Davis had nothing on my dramatic performances. I had game y'all.

In fact, we have family photos of me as a toddler with a giant grin on my chubby little face with tiny clenched fists raised in the air standing next to my sweet smiling, weary-eyed Momma. Believe it or not, those tiny fists were not clenched out of anger or frustration. According to my Mom, that's just what I would do when I was really, really excited and happy. I was so overwhelmed by the feelings inside of me that I couldn't help myself, and my fists would just rise above my head and shake as I shrieked in joy.

Now, let's be honest - that kid scares the hell out of me.

Like..... are you happy, little girl? Are you sad? Are you mad?

Are you happy about being mad? You sure do look mad....

Um, are you going to kill me in my sleep little girl?

If I was babysitting me, I would have been scared to death, and I'm pretty sure you would have been, too.

MIRROR, MIRROR

Although this seems normal now, with a camera on every phone and digital archives of every moment of our lives, my generation is one of the first to be able to watch ourselves *as children* through the wonder of "home videos". Our parents had pictures and the stories their parents told them, but they couldn't hear their own little voice, laugh, or see how they interacted with the world around them. But when Sony introduced the first Camcorder in 1983, my Dad absolutely bought himself that giant black box and mounted it onto his shoulder like he was filming for National Geographic. The Walker home went full VHS.

It's a crazy experience to be able to see and hear yourself as a child. One afternoon I stumbled upon a collection of videos of me at about three years old. I didn't know when I pushed that tape in, that it would kickstart one the greatest revolutions of my life.

It was a crackling video of me "performing" in our old living room through dance, song and dramatic monologue. As a frustrated, pent-up woman in my 20s, I almost didn't recognize myself.

There was this tiny spitfire of a person whirling, singing, laughing and joking on that fuzzy video screen that just blew my mind.

You see, like many of you, I had spent my entire life

26

fighting desperately to CHANGE pretty much everything about myself. I learned quickly that all of my natural instincts were "wrong". I was chronically "wrong" in a world of people pleasers and perfectly behaved ladies that marched militantly under the law that you **never** made anyone **uncomfortable.** I found early on that an emotional, impassioned young woman did not make friends easily.

Desperate to find some connection with the world, I dedicated myself to smoothing out my rough edges. I would try to tame my wild heart, make myself more likable, and reign in my strong opinions and giant dreams. Constantly bumping in my head was - "No one can handle all of me - the real me. I'm way too much!"

And then the follow up punch of "I'm not enough. I don't have what they want. They will never pick me." would knock me to the floor. I was confused, conflicted, and lonely as hell - but at least I had a group to sit with at lunch in high school.

Sis, I am here to say that a life lived in this kind of repression resulted in a frustrated, unsatisfied, lost and lonely grown woman. A woman who was the polar opposite of that tiny three-year-old-spitfire on the fuzzy video screen. I watched that little girl in awe, and something inside of me began to ache.

You see, the three year old me on that screen didn't know to alter her personality, smooth out her dance moves, or tone down her excitement so people would like her more, so they would be more comfortable in her presence.

Nope: three-year-old-Abbi was unapologetically excited, wild-eyed and passionate. She was fully ALIVE. Joy radiated from her chubby little face, and without hesitation she shared that joy, excitement, and herself with anyone who would listen.

Unfortunately, for the fine art of dance, she also liked to mix four-square clogging with hip-hop back spins and ballet. But homegirl didn't care a wink what anyone thought, and she was the most spectacularly beautiful thing I had ever seen.

As I watched, I was so awestruck by that little spitfire of joy (and her awful dance moves), that I just cried. I wasn't even totally sure why. Deep sadness and tears welled up in my heart and eyes, and a grief rose so powerful that it took my breath away - a grief for something I hadn't even known I had lost.

Who was that little girl, and where did she go?

I didn't know how I lost her or how I would ever find her again, but what I did know is that I loved her something fierce.

That little girl was FREE. That little girl knew who the hell she was, and she thought everything about herself was awesome. She didn't second guess herself or clamor for the approval of others. She confidently and unapologetically went forth in life, dance and dramatic monologues, and something inside of me knew the world needed her.... that *I* needed her.

For the first time in my entire life, I saw a picture of myself as FREE. Free from caring about what people thought of me, free from hesitation. I was free to express who I really was and how I truly felt. I could actually *see* me- being fully myself, AND being loved for who I really was, not who I had made myself to be.

The image of that wild-eyed, happy three year old haunted me through my 20s as I searched desperately for the real me, and who I wanted to be. I wept often for that little girl, convinced I had lost her forever. I envied her freedom, and I ached for her JOY.

That fuzzy, dusty video became the catalyst for one of the greatest works in my life: learning to accept, love, care for and celebrate the real ME- ALL of me.

NO MORE

I have a lot inside of me, and like many of you, I have never been quite sure of what to do with all of it. This overwhelming depth of emotion, passion and strength as a woman has caused me countless losses, fights and problems.

This world can be a highly dangerous place for the sensitive heart of a high-strung woman. We are so strong, and yet we are so sensitive.

My heart grieves deeply for the countless "casualties of the soul" in my fellow high-strung sisters who are made for greatness, but who have been silenced and sidelined by rejection, misunderstanding and the pressure to force themselves into the narrow black box of female identity today. I believe that is nothing short of a tragedy. For these women have the insight, creativity and strength of soul that God wants to use to change our world in amazing ways.

So after more than 30 years of my own inner turmoil, loneliness and fear of my own strength, today I say for myself, and for my sisters: NO.MORE.

No more walking in crippling shame and loneliness because I am misunderstood. No more mistreating myself and trying to force myself to be less passionate, to care less, or to be a more "stable" woman so that people will like me better. No more being afraid of my own strength. No more shame. No more believing that everything about me is wrong.

No. HELL NO.

The days of playing small and living at war with ourselves are OVER.

Starting today, you and I will learn to celebrate the rare and incredible gift God has given us in our passionate personalities. We will learn to direct and master our emotions and strength to do incredible things. We will no longer fear them, we will be empowered by them.

We will learn to repent of the unkindnesses we have done to ourselves and others out of misplaced passion, and most importantly, we will learn to love ourselves **well**.

The journey of a High Strung Woman has in many ways been an undocumented and unsupported one, but my heart here is to at least start the conversation. I'm so incredibly humbled and honored that you would pick up this book. It certainly isn't an expert's manual for how to be a great woman, or a professional's guide for how to be a great High Strung Woman. This is simply the story of an over-zealous, spirited, high-strung woman who stumbled and fought her way out of suffering and into a place of peace and power.

This book is NOT about overcoming your high strung spirit, but it IS about finally respecting and caring for one of the greatest gifts God could have given you. I promise you will need the strength of spirit you have been given to do the things He has called you to do. So it's high time we learn to care for it.

This little book is the true story of a 4th Generation Baptist Pastor's Daughter with a wild heart and high-strung personality trying to find her way to authenticity and freedom.

I pray that in some way God uses this book to break loose some chains on your beautiful, wild soul my Sister.

"They are angry with me, because I know what I am."
Said the little eagle.

"How do you know that they are angry with you?"
Said the old owl.

"Because they despise me for wanting to soar, they only want me to peck at the dirt, looking for ants, with them. But I can't do that. I don't have chicken feet, I have eagle wings."

"And what is so wrong with having eagle wings and no chicken feet?"
Asked the old owl.

"I'm not sure, that's what I'm trying to find out."
Said the little eagle.

"They hate you because you know that you are an eagle and they want you to think you are a chicken so that you will peck at the ground looking for ants and worms, so that you will never know that you are an eagle and always think yourself a chicken.

Let them hate you, they will always be chickens, and you will always be an eagle. You must fly. You must soar."
Said the old owl."

— C. JoyBell C.

CHAPTER 2
"AIN'T NO SHAME IN MY GAME...ANYMORE."

#proudtobeahighstrungwoman

Alright Sis. First things first. A High Strung Woman can look and sound a lot of different ways, so don't worry if that particular phrase doesn't resonate with you, or describe you exactly. (Especially if someone gave you this book!)

No two women are the same, and to try to classify ourselves into categories works against the very foundation of this book. Who you are is unique, and you should be 100 percent the real *you*. Learning about and loving all of who you really are is a life-long study, and it will never be exactly the same for any two women.

So, here's the deal. If you read something in these pages that resonates with your soul, grab onto it and glean every bit of truth and insight that you can. But don't you dare be afraid to release it if you find it no longer is in agreement with who you are, or if you find that your version is slightly different. You alone can know the real you, and it is only in really knowing ourselves that we can learn to truly care for ourselves and rock what we've got.

This is about becoming more *you* - not more like anyone else, even if at times it may seem extremely helpful. It won't serve you in the long run, trust me.

So with that being said, a High Strung Woman can have many different names and ideas wrapped around her. A few of which just might include:

"Emotional, intense, sensitive, drama-queen, loud, quiet, harsh, perfectionist, driven, control freak, Type-A, critical, passive-aggressive, or just out-right aggressive, dramatic, manipulative, backseat-driver, helicopter-mom, controlling, alpha-female, spirited, uptight, firecracker, pistol, and the ever popular but not so nice …. "Bitch".

No matter what name others have spoken over you, I believe that what connects us in this place of being high-strung is that it all boils down to the PASSION in our souls- *we feel things strongly, we care deeply, and ultimately we operate at a very high internal level.*

However you express it, (which can be loud or even silent) the root of our high-strung spirit is that we feel things deeply, and that STUFF MATTERS to us!

Hell, let's be honest: EVERYTHING MATTERS to us, and no, we can't turn it off.

Now listen, when we don't understand what's going on inside of us, chances are we will wear ourselves and everyone else around us plumb out. Can I get a witness? (That's church talk for "Can I get a 'hell yeah'?")

I have done it, I have lived it, and I have cried over it. *A lot.*

Y'all, there were seasons in my life when my own friends and family straight up RAN when they saw me coming, especially after a bad spell.

To hold in what I was feeling felt like I was drowning inside. So in a panic to "breathe" I expressed how I felt, blurted out what I thought and pushed for what I needed from anyone around me. It was an act of desperation- to survive what was happening to me, inside of me.

I took my inner turmoil and handed it over to the outside world through expression in an attempt to snatch a breath from under the crashing waves of my emotions. In my experience I literally have never gotten exactly what I wanted and needed from those around me in response to my panicked expression.

It's not the outside world's job to settle our inner storms, to validate our hurts, or affirm our offenses. When we come to them in a wild vulnerable state demanding they do something that they just can't- we leave alone, ashamed, and wounded. We'll talk more about this later- but there is another powerful option for honoring our feelings besides blurting them all out or stuffing them all down. We must be able to express our feelings, but we've got to learn a better way.

I seemed to find the most trouble, as well as my deepest hurts and rejections, when I expressed by big feelings.

When my unfiltered, desperate expressions of how I felt came roaring forth (because I felt like I couldn't breathe-remember?) they always seemed to scare and hurt those I loved. As they distanced themselves, I was left neck deep in shame, deep loneliness, and a suffocating embarrassment.

When I tried my other option - stuffing down all of my feelings - it left me in deep anger, sadness and eventually depression. Refusing to feel or acknowledge my feelings only made my emotions stronger and more intense. Emotions are like water. You cannot bottle them up forever. They *must* have somewhere to go. We reach a breaking point, and an outburst cannot be contained. As I am sure you've experienced, the outbursts of our repressed emotions are always far bigger and more intense than their original form. It's like they grow at radioactive speed when we hide them in the dark.

But this book that you hold in your hands today is about our radical HOPE: finding freedom and JOY as a woman with strong emotions, a powerful personality, and getting to walk out the incredible calling on our lives by being our truest selves. This life is waiting for us, and oh, Sis, is it so good.

We have been given something absolutely incredible in our high-strung spirit, because it reflects the Glory of the One who made us! We just haven't learned how to properly respect and care for it quite yet. We're like a student driver behind the wheel of a Lamborghini, and we simply don't know what to do with all that power, much less know how to properly take care of it.

Sis. Seriously. *No **wonder*** we've flattened more than a few people crossing the street, destroyed road barricades and wrecked flying around corners! We simply need more training, a deeper understanding and better tools to be able to master the magnificent engine we've been given.

This incredible strength of soul, and the strength of spirit that we have within us is an awe-inspiringly powerful force. We can do things no one else can, and, make no mistake about it, we are a force to be reckoned with.

We can either choose to keep complaining about our Lamborghini engine, mistreating it and being frustrated by it's excessive strength, or we can begin to see it for what it is - a beautiful, powerful, incredibly special masterpiece - handcrafted by our Creator to do things that no one else can.

Like any great natural force, our strong spirit can be used to do incredible things, or it can be used to cause unimaginable destruction.

Unfortunately, we usually only realize how strong we are and how deep it runs within us in through the destruction - when our sharp tongues and frustrated hearts bring grown men to tears and shame, when we emotionally explode at our children or spouses with such force that they cower in fear from us, or even when we manipulate people around us to try to get love, affirmation and companionship because we are so desperate for connection.

THIS is usually the point where shame comes to reign in our hearts.

"I am a bad, angry woman. I cannot control what goes on inside of me, and I hurt people when I feel things."

So what do we do? What can we do?

We can eat all of the chips and queso, ice cream and chocolate in the Northern Hemisphere, we can binge watch Netflix until they finally stop asking us if we are, in fact "still watching," or we can become a master mixologist at all types of cocktails - including ones made of tiny pastel pills to numb our pain.

But what we seem to do the most is shut off all of our feelings and wrap ourselves in shame to make sure nothing escapes from us ever again.

We truly don't want to hurt those we love, and Lord knows we are tired of hurting ourselves.

Embarrassed, bloody from self-inflicted wounds and deeply ashamed, we shut it all down.

For most of my life, I thought that this was the only way to protect people, to protect myself and ultimately make myself more lovable.

MY GIRL ELSA

I'll never forget the first time I saw the movie Frozen. It was practically a spiritual experience full of revelation, truths and a new sisterhood. Isn't that what you expect when you watch a Disney movie?

When Elsa found her inner ice super power and couldn't control it, she hauled it on up to the mountain and made herself an ice fortress. She lived alone to protect those she loved from her uncontrollable force, and I was like... "YAAAAAS GURL."

For the first time in my life, I thought, "Maybe I am a Disney Princess after all... Just the one that can freeze the entire world in a nanosecond and must live in complete isolation in order to protect the universe." But can I still get the Disney princess hair and dress?

Listening to Idina Menzel belt out "Let It Go," my heart was like:

"ELSA- GIRL!!!!! I too, have this crazy secret super power that I can't control! All I want is connection and love, and to go sing and build a snowman with my little sister in the magical forest filled with happy Disney woodland creatures- but I never know when my secret power will come flying out of my mouth and hurt someone! So girl- can I come live in your Ice Castle?"

What a masterful plan of the enemy to take out one of God's most amazing, anointed and powerful creatures - the High Strung Woman. All he has to do is convince us that we are shameful, angry and unstable women, and we will **_take ourselves out_** of the game of life.

YOU ARE STRAIGHT ROYALTY

Alright sis, let's get real honest here: I don't know where you personally stand with God, Jesus, or "church" things. You do NOT have to agree with me on every point to benefit from this book. But just so you know where I am coming from, let me lay it out real quick.

I believe with every fiber of my being that God Almighty created everything we see and even beyond, and that because He created it, He reigns as King over all of it- both the physical world and the spiritual. He handcrafted every single one of us, because He loves us fiercely and delights in us as His creation. This is important to me, and also for you to know about me, because it was in knowing that **_God made me, designed every part of me on purpose,_** that led me to such a deep healing love and appreciation for my real self.

Now stick with me here: because God is perfect, but we are obviously not, we stand separated from Him. We're not separated from Him because He is mean, but because He is holy- and our imperfections, our sin simply cannot stand in His presence. BUT He loved us so much, and wanted us so badly, that He made a radical way to unite us again by removing our sins. God sent His son Jesus to live a perfect life here on earth and then die on the cross to pay for our sins- to remove them, so that we can now know Him deeply, walk with Him in this life, have access to His power here on earth, live life on a whole other level, and finally be with Him in heaven forever. When we accept what Jesus did for us by paying for our sins, we see how much He loves us and we now have unlimited access and relationship to the KING of the Universe!!

Bottom line: I believe our **lineage is royalty** Sis. We are daughters of the King Of The Universe. And who the hell wouldn't want to find out she is royalty? Because whether you know it or not, you **are royalty,** Sis. It's high time we live like it.

I also believe we have a very real enemy that hates God and thus hates us, and he wants to keep us convinced that we are not eagles, as the ending story by C. Joybell C. from Chapter 1 says, but that we are just small, insignificant chickens. Chickens are not a threat to the enemy's works or his strongholds in this world, but eagles - you bet your ass they make the enemy tremble. Whether you believe in God or have a relationship with Jesus or not, I know that you have seen darkness at work in this world, and that darkness is run by the enemy of our souls. He is a master deceiver, a liar and he works overtime because he knows what's coming. He knows he doesn't win. He knows God does. But that hasn't stopped him from trying every single day to take as many of us down as he can by turning us against God, ourselves and others.

My purpose in saying all of this is simply to remind you that there is a God who is crazy about you and wants to have a close relationship with YOU, as well as to expose the reality, perhaps for the first time, that you have a very real enemy. His goal is to silence you, squelch your dreams and make you SMALL. There is more at work in your life to hold you back than just your own issues. But we don't have to be afraid, because we have a CHAMPION of our soul in Jesus, and He always wins. He delights in you, thinks you are one of the greatest things He ever made and HE HAS GOT YOUR BACK SIS! You have the full weight of His Kingdom supporting you when you walk with Him! The call on your life is profound as a High Strung Woman, and it's time to align with the King Of The Universe.

THE WORLD NEEDS OUR STRENGTH

The assault on our souls as High Strung Women, is *absolutely* a master plan of the enemy - don't you think different for one second. My Dad taught me a few years ago that anything and anyone with power of any kind has a target on their backs in the spirit realm, and you, my sister, hold tremendous power in your soul. It's time we learn to protect ourselves and speak the truth in this place. We don't have to be afraid, but we would be fools to not live aware.

Power and strength are irresistible to the enemy. He is drawn to it, and make no mistake about it - he always tries to make it his own.

This has made generations of well meaning people fundamentally afraid of power. They run from it like the plague, and we have suffered accordingly.

Fearing power is only a half truth. But respecting power and wielding it with responsibility and understanding, that is a full truth.

We all know that a big strong man can defend the innocent or crush those weaker than him to steal for his own gain. The strength is the same, but it is what the man does with his strength that makes him great or not. The strength itself is not a problem, or even something to be feared. But it is the USE of our strength where the responsibility lies. When there is no direction or purpose for strength, abuse seems to follow.

In the places where you have not known what to do with your strong emotions, intense opinions, and fiery passion- have you not found trouble? Lord have mercy, I have.

Strong men and the use of their strength is something we are all very familiar with, but strong women? No. We have shunned, shamed and shut out any idea of strong women, especially in religious communities and the church house.

And Lord have mercy, when our strength does roar forth, they shame us even more. No wonder we are so deeply conflicted!

It is a deep and dark work to convince a strong person that they are weak, that they should fear their strength, and that they should never, ever use it. Call me Pentecostal- I don't even care- cause that lie is straight from the pit of hell. You can shake yo church tambourine and dance on that truth sister.

God Almighty, if He is nothing else, He is the ultimate POWER. He is the ultimate strength. When we walk in the strength He has given us and use it in the right ways, we radiate HIS glory and we become a profound threat to the enemy's plan. No wonder the enemy wants to shut us down.

A strong, powerful woman is a gift to the world around her - just ask those who are loved by her.

Our world desperately needs women to embrace and walk in their power, but with great power comes great responsibility. We are responsible to learn how to care for it, direct it and know it's limits. For only in that place can we properly direct our strength to radically challenge and change our world.

QUESTIONS

- What words or names have others written over you? (Controlling, sensitive, emotional, etc.)

- Where have you experienced how strong you really are?

- Where has your high strung personality caused you trouble?

- Can you identify places or reasons why your enemy would want to keep you small?

CHAPTER 3
LADY MISUNDERSTOOD

"To Be Great Is To Be Misunderstood."
- Ralph Waldo Emerson

When the God of the Universe chose to create you and I as High Strung Women, He gave us a small taste of His own holy passion, His fire and His glory. We were designed for greatness, and yet we have definitely been misunderstood.

I have experienced so much pain, loneliness and shame as a High Strung Woman, and chances are, you're holding this book today because you have too. I never seemed to fit well in any situation. I always seemed to care too much about everything - especially compared to my family, my classmates and my friends. They just didn't get me, and I felt terribly alone.

Always too much, always too strong,
always too emotional.

Everything about me seemed to be wrong, and I hated it. In these moments of intense pain and loneliness, we turn on ourselves.

I know I turned my back on the bright-eyed little girl with unorthodox dance moves, yelling over my shoulder that she was way too much, and if she ever wanted to be liked, she better learn to TONE IT DOWN. She needed to stuff down all of her passion, her excitement, and her strength and become less threatening if she wanted to have any friends.

It's a tragic day in the life of a High Strung Woman when we betray our true self, and it *always* costs us so much more than we realize.

One of the seasons that is hardest for me to watch on our home videos, is 10-year-old me. The light is gone from my eyes, I am overwhelmingly insecure, desperate for attention and affirmation - and most importantly, I can see flickers of my high-strung-spiritedness desperately trying to find places to break through. This usually resulted in over-the-top awkwardness or jokes that weren't funny. I would make cutting and hurtful remarks to my little sister and try to control the situations around me.

At that point in my life, I was the eldest Pastor's daughter to a large congregation. Thousands of eyes were constantly watching and evaluating me, reporting my every move to my parents.

For most kids, trying to please their parents is burden enough. But I had several hundred sets of parents that wanted me to be an example for their own kids, so they pushed me and my family, accordingly. I was a good little soldier and rose to the challenge. I followed all of the rules and was generally well liked, so long as I did what was expected of me.

But the truth is I never felt safe. I knew my parents loved me. I thought Jesus loved me. But people? No. Their opinions changed every hour, and it all depended on how they felt about me that day. And yet, I died a thousand deaths for them, because I wanted them to love me so badly.

Three-year-old Abbi lived out of her true self, but ten-year-old Abbi had become deeply entrenched in living for the approval of others. You can see the physical changes on my face, and it just breaks my heart. What a tragedy. I feel so much grief for that little girl. I can close my eyes and feel the loneliness, awkwardness and desperation of that ten-year-old. I can feel it because I know it all too well as an adult.

On the rare occasion that my true self came roaring forth, it was always met with big eyes, misinterpretation and instant

44

rejection as I painfully watched those I loved distance themselves from me after an outburst.

It is no secret that we tend to judge that which we do not understand.

But I've found that we can often be the hardest on the ones that are most like us, because they remind us of parts of ourselves we have silenced, mutilated and denied. And we don't like to be reminded.

Some of the most critical women on the planet, myself included, can be High Strung Women getting after other High Strung Women.

Hell may hath no fury like a woman scorned, but if you scorn a High Strung Woman in a point of vulnerability, hell will seem like a cakewalk.

When we are scorned, we then most often turn to scorning.

Here's how it seems to happen.

In a moment where our true selves break through, we challenge the rules and rattle well-behaved-lady protocol. The lady gatekeepers won't stand such an upset, and so we are scorned: reprimanded, rejected, and outcast, to re-establish the group dynamic.

Embarrassed, ashamed and angry, we vow to never, ever feel this way again.

Here's the craziest part: We don't get mad at the lady gatekeepers for scorning us. Instead, we turn on ourselves. We convince ourselves that it's our fault we are being rejected, and we double down to make ourselves follow their rules and never step out of line again. We become so dedicated to following the rules to avoid pain, that before we know it- we've become another enforcer of the scorning. The same scorn that wounded us so deeply and shut us down, we now push on others.

It takes a wild and daring soul to be willing to be outcast in exchange for personal authenticity. And yet, an authentic woman will know more love, satisfaction and community than the lady gatekeepers' groups could ever dream of. That brave woman will be all of who she is and she will know great joy and real relationships because of it. Everything else is just pretend built on pretend.

Mean Girls is one of those movies that is so accurate at times that you just cringe. I mean, I think it better describes grown women than just teenage girls most of the time. Let's be honest y'all - we are awful to each other... and it's most often because we are awful to ourselves.

Becoming an enforcer of scorn and shame can sneak in on us. In my head it often sounded like: "What? Who the hell does she think she is? We can't do that. We're not allowed to do that. She's NOT allowed to do that. Doesn't she know she can't do that? Somebody better get her ass in line." (Insert death stare here.)

As women, we are very quick to evaluate...uhm, *judge*, the world and the people around us. It's like somewhere we got a hold of this idea of "women's intuition" and saw it as a golden opportunity to pass on all our judgements without any consequences.

Somehow, this seems to turn us into the "hall monitors of LIFE." It's so easy to slip into, and I can tell you, although it feels satisfying at times to make sure the rules are followed, or more accurately - that you are RIGHT (and safe, and unattackable etc.), it's a miserable existence. There is NO life there in the long run.

Sisters, we are here to lay down our hall monitor badges and our tools of self inflicted pain, and step into all that we are. The incredible thing is that only then can we find the grace to let others be who and where they are as well. By daring to be the real us, we give others permission to be the real them.

Hey Sis: you CAN sit with us, and we want to hear your story!

IN THE HANDS OF A MASTER

Think of some of the greatest natural forces in our world: fire, water, wind.

These forces have unmatched earthly power. They can cause massive death and destruction through wildfires, hurricanes, and tornadoes, but when they are harnessed, the exact same power can do incredible things. Things that build up and give life.

Fire is a great example. Unharnessed - fire can be excessively powerful and destructive. Just take one look at the footage of a wildfire raging and swallowing up homes. It will take your breath away. It moves faster than you can seem to see it, and it leaves nothing but death and destruction in its wake. If left unchecked, the fire will destroy everything around it, and eventually even itself by burning out.

But in the care of a Master, fire can do incredible things that nothing else can.

When humans learned how to harness and properly care for fire, it changed our lives forever. Fire brought light to dark nights, warmth to freezing places, and it changed what and how we ate.

The same is true of your spirit my Sister - in the hands of a Master, you can do incredible things that no one else can.

Listen Sis, we are going to learn how to care, and care well, for our high-strung spirit like a Master. We are going to learn to respect and direct our strength to do the brave things God has called us to do with all of the authority of heaven.

By refusing to be anything other than our real selves, and by choosing authenticity over perfection every single day, we will give every woman we come in contact with permission to be her true self and perhaps lend her the courage to start showing up as her right now.

Let this be our prayer:
This is my aim, this is my plea: draw me to Thee, ever more, help me be me.

QUESTIONS

- Where have you been misunderstood?

- Have you become an enforcer of the scorning?

- Where can you choose authenticity over perfection in your life today?

- How will your world benefit from you being the real you? (Hint: here are some of the reasons why the enemy wants to take you out.)

- How can you dare to show up as the real you today?

CHAPTER 4
GENTLE AND QUIET SPIRIT? UH, NOPE.

G ather round now girls, let me tell you a story.
I grew up as a Pastor's daughter in deep Texas- the oldest of 3 kids, with a massive church of thousands watching my every move. Literally - Every.Freaking.Move. The first time I held my middle school boyfriend's hand, someone had already called my parents and told on me by the time I got home. (It was at a Jaci Velasquez concert at the church- of course- and I lived seven minutes away.)

Now, as if that kind of life wasn't dramatic enough, I am actually also a fourth Generation Southern Baptist's Preacher's Daughter. What on earth does all that mean? Well, that means my Daddy, Grand-Daddy and Great Grand-Daddy were all Southern Baptist Preachers for all, or most of their lives.

That means one entire side of my genetic lineage's "family business," as my husband calls it, is CHURCH. The family *business* is **church**.

Lawwwwd have mercy on us all. We sound like a wild time don't we?

In case you are not familiar with church people, let me give you a little idea of what we're dealing with here.

Southern Baptists are typically highly conservative and fundamentally fearful of all that's not explicitly in the Bible.

They are also known worldwide for their disapproval of fun. (Family legend has it that a distant relative in Mississippi was kicked out of their Southern Baptist home church for attending a barn raising where there was *dancing*. Come Lord Jesus.)

Okay, so that's not *all* true, Southern Baptists can also be some of the most generous, funny, kind-hearted, deeply loyal and genuine people you will ever meet. Nevertheless, I found some of my deepest rejection from church people. You can love your family with everything you've got and still carry wounds from your experiences with them. Our wounds and scars shape our stories, and these have shaped mine.

If you haven't spent any time in the South, first of all, let us say, "Bless your heart," because it's a truly special place filled with spirit, loyalty and celebration. I must also say that the South has a complicated and dark history: one that grieves my heart deeply, especially with such long running horrors like racism and social injustice. And yet, the Southern culture is a big part of my story, and so I share.

Southern Women are a sight to behold, and a force to be reckoned with. Their beauty, charm, and manner is known throughout the world.

Imagine the most beautiful, sweet smelling and inviting flower you've ever seen. As you step in closer, breathe in that sweet fragrance, and soak in the beauty of the vibrant colors of the petals, you come to realize that at the heart of that flower, hidden behind it's beauty, is a legit stick of dynamite. Now, you don't see a lit fuse, or hear a ticking clock attached ready to explode- so there's not necessarily any pressing danger, but a wise person would simply proceed with caution.

That, my dear friends, is a Southern Woman: dynamite disguised as a garden flower.

Beauty, grace, charm and intelligence wrapped around a firecracker of spirit, loyalty, femininity and belief. She is a wondrous thing to behold, but you do not want to cross her.

That's just a Southern Woman- a Southern *Baptist* Woman is

50

a whole other phenomenon, wrapped in faith, tradition, religion, and protocol- but for times sake- just know this...

There is absolutely a right and a wrong way to be a woman in the South - especially in the church house.

It was around these women, in this place, that I first experienced the pressure to change myself, to conform and to be anything but the real me.

I grew up in Texas which some do not consider the true "South." But the Southern Baptist Women in Texas seemed to follow Southern church lady protocol. When you also consider that I have generations of family from Mississippi, you can see that this girl got it from all sides.

Now, NO ONE loves to throw around Scripture about what a "Godly woman" is quite like the Southern Baptists. Southern Baptist ladies can and will straight up LADY-SHAME you when you step out of line - and they'll do it with a smile on their face, a Bible verse on their pink lips and a casserole in their hand.

Their founding creed seemed to be taken out of 1 Peter 3:3-4, where Scripture is speaking directly to women...

"Your adornment must not be merely external - braiding the hair, and wearing gold jewelry, or putting on dresses; but let it be the hidden person of the heart, with the imperishable quality of a gentle and quiet spirit, which is precious in the sight of God."

Oh, how I hated this verse.

Let's be honest Sis, this Biblical description of what it means to be a woman sounds like the worst thing EVER. It's extremely non-JLo, and it felt suffocating and oppressive to my wild heart. But Lord have mercy, the "gentle and quiet spirit" is a big freaking deal to the church people.

I heard that verse out of 1 Peter 3 more than I ever wanted to, and it seemed to shout that everything I was drawn to, and everything that came naturally to me was WRONG.

For starters:

"Your adornment must not be merely external - braiding the hair, and wearing gold jewelry, or putting on dresses..."

Oh, hell.

Sis, I LOVE me some big hair, giant gold jewelry and fun clothes. LOVE THEM. I have too much of all 3 of those things- and in complete joy and excess, I have and love them.

This is not looking good for ol' Ab.

Second of all:

"But let it be the hidden person of the heart, with the imperishable quality of a gentle and quiet spirit, which is precious in the sight of God."

This was the nail in the coffin. There's not a damn thing about me that is gentle or quiet. Not a dayyyyuuuuummm thing.

No matter how hard I tried to beat myself into submission, every time I heard that verse, my soul cringed. I HATED it, because it seemed to confirm one of my greatest fears: that even God Himself thought I was too much. The church ladies absolutely thought I was too much, and they made sure I knew it. I was miserable, trying as hard as I could and mad as hell all at the same time.

To make matters worse, I was also convinced that somehow these weirdly powerful church ladies also held the keys to my happiness in love. I was convinced that if I could make myself "gentle and quiet" enough, that I would finally earn, uh, "find" my husband. (Bless. Bless my dumb little heart.)

I mean, every good church lady knows that good, godly men don't like "spirited women" as wives. As lovers, sure. But you better keep it between the lines of propriety if you want him to put a ring on it and marry you in the church house in front of your friends and family.

I spent years of my life trying to win over those damn church ladies, trying to tame my wild heart, and in the end I honestly found myself hating everyone, but especially women. From where I sat they were the ones tormenting and rejecting me. I was exhausted and had never felt more alone.

(IMPORTANT SIDE NOTE: Down the road I realized

that I would rather be an old spinster with a house full of stinky cats than marry one of those horrid legalistic church men that I thought I could "earn" with a gentle and quiet spirit, I set on out happily chasing down life on my own, and ended up marrying a man who loves Jesus and the real me. He celebrates me, brings out my wild heart, strong spirit, and makes me better every single day. He is my greatest gift, and I am forever grateful that God gave me a man that loves the real ME- but that only happened after I started showing up in this life AS the real me.)

Now, back to my point - when you spend every waking moment of your life trying to change everything about yourself, second guessing every decision in hopes that it will make people like you better, it's just a matter of time before you pretty much lose your damn mind.

In my life, it has been at these significant breaking points when I finally have no choice but to be fiercely honest and face myself and my God.

Exhausted from the war with myself- I finally turned to Him and pretty much said …

Hey God? Apparently everything about me is wrong, according to- well, everyone, but I'm also pretty sure that You made ME - all of me exactly like this - crazy over-the-top emotional, passionate, sensitive, intense and all, Sara Abigail Walker. So I'm gonna need to work this out with You, because I am so beat up I can't even crawl across the floor at this point. I promise I can learn to trust You. I can learn to tune out the other voices. But I am going to need to hear from YOU. Help. Help me please.

Because He is a good, good Father to His daughters, He answered, in power and mercy, to my weary, bloody heart.

JESUS IS NOT THE CHURCH,
NOR THE CHURCH LADIES.

I won't lie, it took me a long time, but after a lot of good therapy and more than a few come-to-Jesus-meetings with the REAL Jesus, I finally embraced my high strung spirit and I feel closer to God than ever before. I can now see His power in and through me in ways that make my heart sing, and I am walking in an authority and confidence that can only come from knowing who you are, and that who you are is GOOD. God says what He made in me was GOOD, and I now trust Him. Anyone who feels differently about me can just work it on out.

Over the last decade, one of the greatest truths I've learned is that Jesus is NOT the same as the church, nor their well meaning, but often sharp-tongued sisters and brothers. The church is full of *humans*. And as warm hearted, and well-meaning as they may be, they are HUMAN nonetheless. Humans can misinterpret, wound, confuse and reject you. But Jesus, He misinterprets NOTHING, and His heart is always to draw us home to His love.

It's extremely important to me that you hear this: We don't throw out the church or it's people because of it's inevitable humanity. NO. Rather, we must approach it with realistic expectations and understanding - always looking to Jesus alone for the real TRUTH and extending grace to the humanity of all things.

The pressures you face to change, censor, or limit yourself may not come from your church, or spiritual community. They may come from your family, your husband's family, your industry, social media, or your culture. But no matter where they come from, you are not meant to be caged, dear one. We must relentlessly pursue freedom and truth.

If you'll stick with me, I'm about to share some major revelations in my life that God used to bring the kind of radical FREEDOM that our wild hearts long for!

QUESTIONS

• Where have you experienced the most rejection as a high strung woman? (Your family? Your Industry? Your Relationships? Get specific.)

• Where or how have you experienced the most pressure to change yourself, become less like you, and more like a group or ideal?

• What lies have you believed about yourself?

• How do you think God feels about the real you?

CHAPTER 5
"THAT'LL PREACH"

"Great spirits have always encountered violent opposition from mediocre minds."
-Albert Einstein

inding freedom from the expectations and pressures of others is paramount in the life of a High Strung Woman. If we don't relentlessly pursue and live out of this radical freedom from what others think of us, we will be stuck in a frustrating cycle. We will take one step forward toward our true selves, and when it's not met with approval, we'll take 2 steps back, apologizing for who we are.

God used two very important things in my life to free me of this heaviness of other people's expectations and opinions.

First, I finally realized that the church ladies, or anyone else who felt the need to criticize my personality, spirit or life choices at the moment, could just take their concerns straight on to the Good Lord Himself.

Despite the sheer panic that can still rise in my heart when I hear the hen cackling of gossip spreading through a room, I have learned that I can, in fact, trust HIM with my reputation. No matter what they disapprove of - He is a big enough GOD to handle it, to handle THEM. I can trust HIM with their criticisms, release them to Him to deal with (not just randomly release them - that never works), and I really never have to pay attention to them again. He is a big enough God to handle the church ladies. He is a big enough God to handle your Mama, your co-workers and your family.

God can handle anyone who has an opinion about you.

Hallelujah, y'all. **That'll preach.**

*"That'll Preach" is something we say in the Southern Churchhouse when we hear something really, really good. It means that what you've just heard is a truth so strong, and so deep on so many levels that it could preach it's own sermons for a hot-minute. It's a truth that rattles your soul and stirs your spirit.

LIDA THE YODA

The second powerful thing God used to set my heart free also showed me what a big sense of humor God has.

During my tormented mid-20s while I was on staff at my Dad's church, a tiny little white-haired woman named Lida Smith agreed to mentor me.

I have a lot of amazing women in my life, for which I am deeply grateful, but Lida Smith very well may be the most incredible woman to walk this earth. For starters, she is the cutest, most hip little Grandmother you've ever seen. She wears fun, trendy glasses that perfectly compliment her sassy white hair. She makes enchiladas that feed a part of you that you never thought could be full, and her sweet voice calms your very soul with just a few words. With so much chaos raging inside of me, I decided Lida was my lighthouse in the storm. She was going to be my Holy Grail for that damn "gentle and quiet spirit" I had to have, and so I gathered up my courage and my crazy and asked her to mentor me.

Why? Because I had never seen Lida out of control. I had never seen her angry. I had never seen or heard her say anything out of place, and I had known her for as long as I could remember. She was the Director of Women's Ministry for my Dad's church, and from my perspective, she was I Peter 3 incarnate. She was everything I thought I was supposed to be - sweet, kind hearted, and quiet-mannered. You know, the things that God, and apparently men, loved.

If I'm honest I was hoping that if I just sit close enough to her for long enough, that maybe her gentleness would rub off on me.

But, ya'll. The funniest thing happened as we met weekly to talk and pray.

This tiny soft spoken, white-haired woman *shocked me*. She wasn't some sheepish, churchy, Stepford wife. Nope.

Lida was a damn pistol.

She had fire in her belly, the heart of a warrior and she wouldn't back down unless God Himself told her to. I was convinced even then she could probably talk Him out of it! She was so fierce of spirit that it intimidated me at times, and I adored her.

As we wrestled through my many issues, most often my excessive "strength of spirit" problems, one day she looked calmly into my eyes, and simply said the word, *"Meekness."*

I recoiled immediately, and I probably would have hissed out loud if I didn't think someone in the church office might try to pin me down, anoint me with oil and pray a demon out of me. (It's funny because it's true.)

"Here we go again. I'm going to have to abandon every natural thing about myself. I will have to beat myself into that small, humiliating box so I can finally be gentle and quiet." Meekness? Ugh. I hated that word.

Meekness sounded like someone who couldn't look another person in the eye, someone beaten down, unworthy, defeated, and humiliated. Surely Lida didn't like that word either?

In her sweet, soft voice, but with all the authority of heaven, she said, "Sweet Abbi, meekness isn't weakness or humiliation. Meekness is great strength under control."

Great strength, under control.

This tiny grandmother in all of her Yoda wisdom broke down a wall in my soul prison with just one sentence. And for the first time in my entire life, I saw light through the dungeon. I saw hope.

You see, I could *hear* the words "great strength under control" from Lida, because she wasn't controlled by anyone or anything. She was wildly free, and audaciously happy. She willingly and happily chose to submit herself to the things she wanted to. She didn't limit herself, but she did control, direct, and harness the greatest strength of spirit in a woman I had ever seen. As if that wasn't impressive enough- she was the happiest, most powerful, and AT PEACE, person I had ever been in a room with.

What makes Lida even more amazing, is that she hasn't led a perfect, charmed life. She experienced heartache, betrayal and humiliation at a level that would make most women lay down and die. She has seen it all, and it hasn't destroyed her, jaded her or made her quit. In fact, she pressed into life harder after her world was torn apart, and y'all, she **glowed**. Her skin literally glowed from how alive her spirit was, and I stood in awe.

When you see someone like this you know you are in the presence of greatness. This is a woman whom God Himself shines through, and I wanted what she had more than anything I had ever wanted in my life.

Power and peace cohabitating in the chest of a woman who radiated happiness.

Sign me up.

POWER AT PEACE

For several years right out of college, I served as the Youth Ministry Director on staff of my Dad's church, and I had a front-row seat to some things I hadn't ever seen before, and will never forget.

At the time, Lida and I were pretty much the only 2 women on the full-time ministry staff, and on more than one occasion, the "men of ministry" couldn't agree on a particular decision. Now, I don't know how much time you've spent with men who are in "ministry" (pastors, associate pastors, ministry directors, speakers, evangelists, writers,) but they are typically extremely ALPHA men, and their confidence is only multiplied by thinking and believing that they hear and are following God Himself. I'm not at all saying that that is a bad thing. We absolutely need confident leadership. But it can also be a dangerous combination in some places. I'll never forget the first time I saw it combust in a church staff meeting.

As a staff, we had spent at least two hours going back and forth on the direction for a big ministry event, and it had gotten heated, to say the least. In the animal kingdom, our meeting room would have looked like the Amazon - a shredded forest of scratched up and "scented" trees, with deafening roars from the competitors as they slapped their chests and showed their teeth- but all in the name of "ministry", of course. These staff guys were all worked up, and I was fairly confident that at any moment a fist fight might break out. (It totally happens y'all, let's not kid ourselves, but that's another book.)

My dad, the senior pastor, called for quiet in the room, and then turned to Lida. He quietly said, "Lida, what do you think?" And the room went radio silent. I mean, 15 seconds ago you couldn't hear anything over the shouting and chest slapping, and now this tiny white-haired lady held that room in reverent silence just by hearing her name.

She took a deep breath and said, "I don't think we have to decide this right now."

And that was that.

In just 10 words, she spoke with more authority and conviction than we had heard all day. Dad agreed, and closed the meeting in prayer.

My mouth was on the floor. What just happened? Lida didn't lecture the men about how ridiculous they were being (although from where I sat they thoroughly deserved it). She didn't push for an agenda. And she didn't have anything to prove. She sat there quietly listening to each side and I am sure she was praying under her breath the entire time.

The respect and admiration that those alpha men had and still have for Lida astounded me, not just as a fellow staff member, but as a woman. The men in that room didn't defer to her because they were afraid of her, in love with her, or even had to for fear of punishment. They deeply respected her because of who she was, because of HOW she was. I had never seen anything like it.

What I had seen, and I'm sure that you have seen before, were women threatening, screaming, manipulating, crying, throwing things and trying to compete with other men, by becoming man-like. I had never seen a woman *be invited* to speak into such a competition and place of heated friction, much less *end the whole damn game* just by being herself.

Power at peace.

It was an incredible example of what a force we can be as women when we embrace all of what we are: fierce and sensitive, strong and tender, powerful and gentle. Trying to compete with men by becoming more man-like only dishonors and demeans us. Both our power and our peace lie in the magic of being a woman.

Loud, striving women let us take heed. THIS is how we make progress in a world that tries every day to keep us small. Not with our shouts and anger, but with our lives, with our character and our examples. Men will only get louder and bigger when we fight their way, but you let loose some of your woman magic- calm, strong words flowing from your insight and wisdom in the face of rage, and they will spook like a kid on Halloween. They will not know what to do with you, and then you get to teach them. Great strength under control.

Confidence is quiet. Insecurity is loud.

GETTING BRAVE ENOUGH TO TAKE A SECOND LOOK

After learning so much from Lida, I reached a point where it really bothered me that what the church had taught me about what it meant to have a "gentle and quiet spirit" didn't line up with my own real life experiences with God. I knew a God who loved me, who delighted in how He made me. But I just couldn't shake their critical interpretation of that verse.

Eventually, I got brave, rolled up my sleeves and dug in. I mean, I got out my giant leather-bound Hebrew-Greek Key Word study Bible, and I Beth-Moored the pants off 1 Peter 3. Not because I was trying to change myself, but because I was now sure of who Jesus really was, and I was also sure that there had to be something really important missing from the "gentle and quiet spirit" teaching as I had heard it. Because it just couldn't be true that you were only supposed to be sweet, soft, and never worked up.

I've learned to never underestimate the power of our perspective- the angle from which we view things. Everyone has a different perspective, as no two people can ever stand in the exact same place at the same time! Where we stand dictates how much we can see, and what things look like from where we are standing. Two people can look at the exact same thing and accurately see two totally different versions. Consider that the next time you feel frustrated- your perspective is 100 percent unique. It's supposed to be!

Our perspective determines what we see and look for in this life.

I grew up already thinking that God and everyone around me thought that I was "too much", so when I heard the "gentle and quiet spirit" verse, it already lined up with the story I had heard and been repeating to myself my entire life. If I am completely honest- it is what I saw and heard in that verse, because it's what I was already looking for in that verse. Like it or not, we need our worlds to make sense - even if it's a miserable one, at least we feel like we understand it.

But after encountering the real Jesus, and women like Lida Smith who were strong and at peace, my perspective had changed, because I had learned something new.

I came back to 1 Peter 3:3-4 and heard these things instead......

"Your adornment must not be **merely** *external—braiding the hair, and wearing gold jewelry, or putting on dresses..."*

First off, praise Jesus and Hallelujah for the word **MERELY**.

"Your adornment must not be MERELY external...."

I read this from the new perspective that Jesus loved and delighted in me, and saw the word MERELY. 1 Peter is saying don't let your beauty, and all of your effort JUST be great hair, big gold jewelry, and fun clothes. He's not saying you can't have them or love them, but he IS saying what we all know to be true- we've got to be more than how we look, and our efforts should reflect the same. Yes Lord. Give us less flashy Instagram celebrities and more stout, brave hearted women who engage in real life.

Then, the big one:

"But let it be the hidden person of the heart, with the imperishable quality of a gentle and quiet spirit, which is precious in the sight of God."

So what does "gentle and quiet" really mean? Not the way the church ladies taught it to me, but what do those words *actually* mean?

First of all, the word **gentle** was most immediately compared to my new jam, "meekness." Because I had learned earlier from Lida that meekness wasn't weakness, but "great strength under control," I didn't hiss and recoil. I smiled and leaned in.

The Greek word for gentle that is used in this verse is described as:

"A condition of mind and heart which demonstrates gentleness not in weakness, but in POWER. It is a virtue born in strength of character."

COME ON WITH IT

A condition of mind and heart which demonstrates gentleness in POWER!!! Yes Ma'am.

Ya'll. Not only did God love me, not only did He delight in me, His heart was to transform my conflict and misery into PEACE with myself. Not by being someone else, but by being the real me. A big part of that peace was accepting that what He had made was GOOD.

To top it all off, my studies on the word *"quiet"* revealed it wasn't about volume level (Thank you Jesus!). It was about being at peace, calm, and at REST. Quiet - like an undisturbed pond - clear, still, and at rest. That's the exact opposite of the suffering I had known- striving, exhausted, and anxious. What a word to my heart!

Power at peace. Rest in my soul. No longer striving. No longer trying to live and make myself small. Instead, resting in the fact that all of who He made me to be is GOOD. I came to celebrate the truth that He gave me some of His own Holy passion and fire, and I pulled my chair up to the table of Mastery.

We have been given an unbelievable gift ladies- it's high time we learn to see it that way.

We're just getting started.

QUESTIONS

- Who do you admire most as a woman? Why?

- Where have you tried to win battles by becoming more man-like? How did that go for you?

- Are you a woman who is walking in her power and at peace?

- Or are you striving, fighting yourself, and worn out?

- How can you start to rest, stop trying so hard, and be at peace with who you really are today?

CHAPTER 6
BELLA THE HIGH STRUNG WONDER DOG

"Sometimes the best therapists have fur and four legs."
-Steve Wentworth

The first Christmas after Ryan and I were married, my Dad bought my Mom a tiny, wild red puppy. My little brother had left home for college that year, and since they were now empty-nesters, my Dad was convinced my Mom needed a new buddy. Plus, WHO can resist a Christmas puppy?

Looking back, it wasn't his best idea. Mamas who have just finished raising three high-strung children are hardly looking for something else to raise - especially not something that poops on their Persian rugs. But it turned out to be an incredible gift after all, just not for my mom. Apparently Shirley (my Mom), CAN resist a Christmas puppy. Ryan and I, however, can NOT.

If you've followed my journey at all over the last 10 years, you know that Ryan and I ended up with that tiny, wild, red puppy. She was a happy fat little Christmas puppy with bells on her collar, so we named her Bella and took her home to our tiny 800 square foot apartment in downtown Dallas.

Bella was a Vizsla – a beautiful, cinnamon-colored Hungarian pointer, bred to be a world class working dog and one of the best breeds for bird hunting. We didn't know anything about her background when we got her, but she was the cutest, most terrible, highest strung little thing we had ever seen. We could not help but love her.

As we attempted to settle into life with a puppy, we quickly found this little red dog was far more than we bargained for. This was no ordinary puppy. Bella was a spitfire.

She could put the Energizer Bunny to shame. She would eat until she could not walk. She had LOTS to say (Vizslas are notoriously vocal) and homegirl was *strong willed*.

We didn't have a yard at our tiny urban apartment, so we had to walk a long historic residential street called Swiss Avenue in Dallas multiple times a day to try to wear her out. It seemed that we walked all day, every day trying to make her too tired to destroy all of our earthly belongings with her razor sharp puppy teeth. Because good Lord, she absolutely could.

To make matters worse, I was beyond panicked that our neighbors would hear her barking and complain to our landlords. We hadn't shelled out the required $600 pet deposit, nor did we want to.

Just a few weeks after we brought her home, Ryan came home from work to find me on the floor sitting up against a wall in our living room, with huge eyes and a look on my face that must have terrified him. New husbands don't always spook so easily, but he wisely heeded the warning. Bella, I'm sure, was chewing on something she wasn't supposed to, and I no longer cared. He took one look at me, with my glassy eyes, dirty hair and defeated position on the floor - picked Bella up, and walked right back out the door. Trying to keep her from destroying our first home had worn me out, and at that moment, I kind of hated her.

I later learned that Ryan carried that tiny bad puppy right into Petsmart, found their on-staff trainer and said, "Listen Ma'am, we really need some help."

We laughed so hard we cried thinking about it later, but Bella tested us in every possible way those first few months.

As we finally learned more about her breed, and just what

we had gotten ourselves into, we were surprised, though not shocked, to learn that the nickname for Vizsla puppies, is, in fact, "little red devils." Yep, that sounded about right.

I won't lie, Vizsla puppies are not for the faint of heart. I mean, they are like tiny wild Tasmanian devils. They bite like baby sharks, bark with the force of a grown dog, sass anyone trying to discipline them, and I swear, they can chew through steel. But they are also the cutest, wrinkliest, brightest blue eyed little puppy chunks you have ever seen. They will curl up on your neck and go to sleep with their hot puppy breath and warm bellies melting your ice-cold heart. God knew what He was doing when He made them so cute - it's the only motivation strong enough to survive their puppy-badness.

We LOVED our Bella, but for months we were deeply frustrated by her, and we were pretty sure that there was just something wrong with her. It was like she had managed to soak up all of the puppy badness from her entire litter, and now Ryan and I were paying for it. There were days I was convinced she had to be possessed by a demon, and I may or may not have prayed over her more than a few times, just in case. If we had owned anointing oil, I would have just dunked her in it. One can never be too careful when it comes to dark spirits.

As we struggled to learn how to care for her and to train her, everything and everyone told us that the answer was to dominate her. "Show her who's boss!" "Be the Alpha!" We tried and tried, but Bella just did not respond to these tactics. To make matters worse - that kind of approach only pushed her farther from us.

We realized that even though she was stubborn and extremely strong willed, she was also tender and very sensitive. Vizslas are considered "soft dogs," which means you can easily break their spirits with excessive force and discipline.

A dog with a broken spirit will tear your heart out. A broken Vizsla is timid, afraid of everything and a shadow of what she was created to be. It's next to impossible to reverse once broken, and so great care must be taken. To bring out the best of a spirited, high-strung, highly intelligent Vizsla, a master must care for her.

Does this sound familiar?

Do you carry wounds, scars or even a broken spirit from the ones who have tried to dominate and silence you? I know that I do.

When we finally learned how best to love and care for Bella, she became a totally different dog. Walks were fine, but we found that off leash play, swimming, hunting and mental stimulation were the best for her. When she got her exercise, was on the right food and felt safe and secure- she was the best dog a girl could ask for. She pretty much just snuggled up next to me and slept all day.

Bella came from an incredible line of world-class canine athletes - hunters, runners and working dogs. She was not created for city life in Dallas, but when she was properly cared for, she became the best little city dog in the world. She got so good at it in fact, that when we visited my parents and she had to be in the backyard with the other dogs, my family would laugh and say - "Look! Bella is playing 'DOG' today!"

Oh, my sweet girl. In many ways, Bella taught me more about being a High Strung Woman than perhaps anyone else. And oh, how I loved her.

She knew exactly who she was - strong, confident and unapologetic of her temperament. That's what made us all love her so fiercely. She was who she was through and through. Her confidence was a stark contrast to my own frustration at a time in my life when I had pretty much lost all sense of myself in trying to please others.

Bella did not play it cool. EVER. She was over the top about pretty much anything - squirrels, food, new people, other dogs, or being separated from us. She would lose her mind with any of these things. The difference was she didn't try to hide any of her feelings about anything.

When we would meet someone out on a walk or go to the

dog park or the vet, I struggled to control her in some ways. I found myself embarrassed and mad at her for not being able to play it cool or for making me look like an incompetent dog owner. She was never out of control and never ever hurt anyone, but she was far from cool, calm and collected.

There were days she made me red-faced-mad, and then one day, I realized that Bella was completely happy with who she was. Her ability not to care what others thought about her made her free in a way I had never known in my entire life. She was just being her, and I was the one bent out of shape for fear of what other people would think.

I just cried and cried when I realized how I had hushed and reprimanded her, and I resolved to be more like my happy, high-strung pup.

We are never happy, or living up to our full potential, when we try to make ourselves something that we're just not. But when we learn how to understand and direct all of who we are, we breakthrough and reach a level of power that we've never known before.

When we took Bella to the mountains of Montana that first summer- people would just stop and stare as her energy, intelligence, and athleticism were on full display. The same things that wore me out in urban Dallas, flashed in glory as she chased marmots, lept over logs, swam across rivers and ran for miles in the backcountry. She was a sight to behold and an incredible example of all she had to offer in the wildness of Montana.

When she was doing what she was made to do, oh the glory! When she was forced into doing what we thought she was supposed to do, oh the suffering.

That'll preach too.

Our wild hearts long to be loved for who we are. We desperately want to have others run alongside us, and us alongside them. For it is in that freedom and full expression of who we are that we have the greatest love to offer this world.

But how can we love anything when we have refused to

love and appreciate ourselves? Your frustration and loneliness are not signs that something is wrong with you. They very well may be signs that something is wrong with the way you are trying to connect with people. True connection and intimacy can never come out of anything but honesty and deep authenticity.

It takes a brave heart to show yourself to the world, and it takes the heart of a lion to share your true self with those you love most.

Be brave my sister. Dare to show the world the real you, every single day. It is worth more than you know.

QUESTIONS

• Where have others tried to beat you down? Dominate your strong spirit? Discourage your strengths?

• Where are you suffering? I.E. Where are you doing what you feel you are "supposed" to be doing or acting, and finding yourself miserable?

• How can you choose to show up as the REAL you today?

- Who is someone who doesn't seem to like your strength?

Consider this: others likely feel threatened because they don't know how to respond to you, or how to interact with you. It feels intimidating and scary to them. You can extend them grace as you learn better how to navigate your world and own your power. Being powerful does not mean we over-power others, being powerful means we know when and where to use our strength, and with whom we can share freely.

- Who is someone in your life who honors and celebrates the real you? Your strengths?

CHAPTER 7
ABANDONING THE WAR WITH MYSELF

"It's okay. You just forgot who you are.
welcome back."

-unknown

I grew up knowing far more about how to change myself, beat myself into submission and find a way to deal with what was dealt to me than I ever knew about how to truly take care of myself.

Like our Bella, most of the advice I got from people were things like "You need to try harder," "Just stop it," or "At least hide it." That only advice pushed me further from myself and others, and left me frustrated, angry, and in pain.

To bring out our best, to celebrate all of who we are, we must first understand ourselves.

We'll never fully understand something that we are judging, so we must start from a place of radical acceptance - not criticism. We must open our hearts to observe and welcome all that we see. We listen without evaluating- so that we can *learn*. This is a wild and rare practice in the divided world we live in today- but the breakthroughs we so desperately need will be made from listening and learning, not from screaming judgements at each other.

Since we have spent a lifetime in judgement, believing that who and what we are is inherently wrong, most of us only know a life in daily conflict with our true selves.

Think about that for a second - in many ways, all we've known is WAR inside us. Conflict, distrust, unrest, friction and insecurities have been our lifelong companions. We have rarely, if ever, felt SAFE. The threat of being found out is always just around the corner. We live every single day in a fight to change ourselves, and the toll of such a war is harsh on the soul. When we believe we are in constant danger of being exposed, we can never let our guard down.

What a horrible way to live.

When we demand that anyone be different from who they really are, we reject them at the most intimate level. It's offensive, vulgar to their Creator and results in deep suffering. I don't just mean judging and trying to change other people here ladies, I mean us.

And you know what? It grieves the heart of God.

We are thumbing our nose at our Creator and saying, "This - what You made, it's not good enough, and I don't like it."

I have practically made a religion out of trying, striving, and fighting to change myself. In every way, I believed I was never enough, and at the same time, I was always way too much.

When we embrace and live out of that kind of inner rejection - that who and what we are is WRONG - we SUFFER. We suffer deep and we suffer long.

Rejecting ourselves is a dangerous foundation, and anything we build on top of that, even things that can be good for us like exercise and healthy eating, are doomed.

Anytime we build on a lie we are in tremendous danger. For in that place, we are in agreement with the enemy. When we believe that what he says about us is true, we open the door for him to build a spiritual stronghold in our hearts and minds. He cannot come in unless we open the door, but when we give him access he can establish habits, beliefs, and triggers that have a *strong hold on us*. Things that we are compelled to do. Where we don't feel like we have a choice that we have to do them.

Here is what the lies can sound like:

Who I am is wrong, not good enough, and I need major improvements in order to ever be loved, celebrated, beautiful, or welcomed in.

Here is the TRUTH:

The God of the Universe handcrafted ME, every single part on purpose and with great delight. My emotional sensitivities, my strength, my sense of humor, my unique gifts and talents, the shape of my body, the color of my hair, and the passion that burns like a fire in my chest - He made it all on purpose, with great care and attention to detail. When my God sees me, the real me- His face lights up in a huge smile, because He loves me, and He is proud of who He made. He delights in who and where I am RIGHT NOW: not 20 pounds lighter, not with less issues or hurts, not as a better version of myself. He thinks I am one of the best things He ever made- as I am RIGHT NOW.

The more we can see that who, how and where we are right now, is not just good, but GREAT - the more we begin to see ourselves as God sees us - worthy of all of the love and goodness in this world. This is where He begins to change our lives as women who have rejected ourselves. God will always lead us to better places, deeper healing and stronger truths, but *we can only start from where we are right now.* He does not despise our beginnings, and neither should we.

Need more than just my word for it? Let's take it on ovaaah to the Good Book.

Psalm 139:13-14

"For you formed my inward parts; you knitted me together in my mother's womb.

I praise you, for I am fearfully and wonderfully made. Wonderful are your works; my soul knows it very well."

What does this verse mean?

The reigning King of the Universe dreamed you up, designed every single part of you, and sent you right to the world that He knew needed you.

Why do we live every single day like we have so much to apologize for, to make up for, and to improve?

If I were to ask you to stop right now and to lay down your weapons and offenses against yourself, and abandon the list of things you think you need to fix… What would your response be?

Could you stop fighting? Could you abandon the war with yourself? Could you let yourself just BE?

I know how I responded to that question: TOTAL.PANIC.

Nope, nope, and noper.

Stop fighting? Stop trying so hard?

HELL NO.

Trying hard made me feel safe. It made me feel like there was something I could do - that I wasn't just a victim to my imperfect body, my high-strung personality, or my many flaws.

I don't think I am alone in that belief. It's as if we as women, have become addicted to trying. Hell, we'll try anything if we think it can help us avoid pain, exposure and rejection: nasty juice cleanses, painful plastic surgery, elite social groups of mean girls, pills that numb us, horrific workouts - you name it. Sure, it's awful. Yes, we feel like we are punishing ourselves and hate our life- but damn it, the world is going to know how damn hard we are trying to change ourselves, to make ourselves more worthy.

We will do anything to keep from being full on, unedited, unimproved - US.

We believe that no one would love the real us, we're not enough. We're not skinny enough, pulled together enough, healed enough, rich enough or successful enough. We also believe no one will love us because we are too much: too strong, too opinionated, too emotional.

So we set out to earn a second rate love by winning them over with how hard we try. We decide there's something endearing about apologizing for who we are, and trying to make ourselves more worthy. But it's not endearing, it's demeaning.

Damn Sis. That's rough.

To be fair - there is a big world making a boatload of cash selling us a "better" version of ourselves. From photo filters to the diet industry, they promise to make us better than who we really are. We are surrounded on all sides, and that battle is fierce.

I realize this may be wildly unpopular to say, but I can't help it.

The enemy wants to keep us wrapped up in, obsessed with and consumed by "self improvement". He wants us distracted by and chasing diets, programs, smaller bodies, and social approval . But the day we truly come to love, celebrate and stand in all that we are as a daughter of the King, the gates of hell will shake, and our world will never be the same.

Never forget, my sisters, our enemy seeks to steal, kill and destroy.

Through our devout and panicked dedication to change ourselves, he steals our days. He steals our purpose, and he steals our joy.

Truly improving ourselves - is about **growing**. Where who we really are is only getting bigger, stronger, and more focused. Growing, healing, and getting stronger should never feel like punishment. There may be times where we are stretched, where we feel like we're breaking, where we have growing pains- but we are not in pain because we are hating parts of who we are. In growth, we can experience pain because we are outgrowing things and having to increase our strength and endurance. Growing pains are a pressure from growing bigger, not the crushing pain of trying to make ourselves smaller.

Where there is punishment there is fear, and where there is fear- we are not walking in love.

Let me be clear here- no one , and I mean NO ONE loves a good self improvement program more than me. A good diet plan, workout program, mastermind class, or self help book are some of my very favorite things. I LOVE them, and I love to learn from experts. These are powerful resources for us WHEN we come to them from a place of loving ourselves and wanting to grow. However, when we come to them from a place of panicked desperation to change ourselves, we are operating in a very negative and unhealthy place.

Fighting to change who we are versus wanting to grow into a fuller, more vibrant version of ourselves are two very different motives- and we will know what we're operating out of by how we feel when we're in them.

Do you view working out as an opportunity to get stronger- loving how it makes you feel, and honoring and blessing your body as you get after it? Or, do you experience working out as a punishment for eating foods you love? Do you push too hard because you hate the extra weight you are carrying? There is a huge difference between the two, and your body responds totally differently to each one.

I cannot express to you the sorrow in my heart when I realized that I lost four years of my life fighting to change my body. 4 DAMN YEARS OF LIFE y'all- because my body had changed, and I was terrified of it being seen. I set my battle against my body instead of FOR my life.

Whenever we find ourselves fighting against things and not FOR things - it's a clear indication that something is off. Our energy is dramatically different when we are fighting against something. It's negative, and it will never carry the same kind of power.

When we are tearing down instead of building up, we are operating in the enemy's mindset. In the enemy's mindset everything is a threat. We are controlling, rigid, and fearful.

You know what God's mindset is? NOTHING IS A THREAT. Nothing can threaten Him, because He rules over all. The biggest fears, challenges, and obstacles in this world are literally God's footrest. He rests His FEET on our mountains. When we live in God's mindset we are not panicked, easily threatened, or desperate to control. We can trust our bodies, we can dare to love ourselves, and we show the world a BIG God when we live in that kind of freedom.

So, my sisters- we have come to the first of many crossroads. We can either choose to keep fighting ourselves, or we can dare to be radical and abandon the war. We can stay on the hamster wheel of self improvement, or follow our Creator down this brilliant path of self care.

Although my hands can still tremble as I write this, I desperately want to be the woman who abandons the war with myself. It's a choice we must make every single day: to give up the battle with our bodies, our emotions, and our minds.

I want to be brave enough to rock the hell out of everything I've got - every pound, every curve, every dimple, every emotion, every dream, every thought and every wrinkle, every single day. That kind of confidence in a woman will open up a whole new world!

So we come back to this striking question:

Will you stop right now and lay down your weapons, your offenses with yourself?

Will you burn your list? Your list of things you think you have to change, to fix so that you can feel more worthy?

Will you dare to stop trying so damn hard and just be still?

Can you stop fighting, and abandon the war with yourself?

I promise, if you will gather your courage and dare to abandon the war, Jesus will meet you in the most incredible way. Your life will go from exhaustion and non-stop hustle, to rest, celebration and POWER from knowing, loving, and caring for the wonder woman that you are.

We are laying down the lies of self improvement to pick up the joys of self care. We are moving from self judgement and fear to FREEDOM, and it IS the TRUTH that sets us free, my sisters. Because above all, this journey is about FREEDOM.

FREEDOM

I thought that freedom would come when my body finally looked the way I thought it had to, when I wasn't so damn zealous about things, when I stopped being so emotional. But it didn't. It didn't come that way because I honestly never arrived. I never got it all right, and yet freedom came.

How many times have we achieved massive feats of self improvement - from paying off debt to losing 50 pounds, and still found ourselves haunted by the ghosts of "you're still not enough?"

Freedom does not come as a result of "perfection".

Naw girl, I'm gonna say that again- freedom never comes as a result of you finally getting it all right.

Freedom comes when our exhausted, raspy voices cry out from the depths of our prison cell, "NO MORE." Freedom comes when we refuse to stop dying a thousand deaths to win people over so they will tell us we are good enough.

When we have beaten ourselves up for so long that we can't trust our own voice, we have to turn to the One who made us, for the truth. We have to stop talking and listen to a higher authority than our own mind.

My conversation with God went something like this....

"Jesus - I know You said that you formed every part of me, but I am so tired... so very tired of fighting myself, so tired of trying to change everything about me. I want to love myself, to feel beautiful, and be confident- but I just can't see it. All I can see is what's wrong with me, so please help me to see myself through YOUR eyes. Open the eyes and ears of my heart to YOUR voice as my Dad who loves me. Help me to hear Your voice, and please, help my heart find rest."

Freedom comes when we abandon the war with ourselves- Freedom comes when TRUTH sets us free. Lies always beat us down, but truth - even when it's painful, will always set us free and bring LIFE.

Here is some TRUTH about you Sis.

Read it, re-read it, read it out loud, soak it in, meditate on it, preach it to yourself, or record your voice saying it and play it over and over again.

We drown out lies by flooding our hearts and minds with what is TRUE,
not just by telling ourselves what is not true.

- You do not need to be changed, nor improved in order to be loved, liked, or worthy. You are incredible exactly as you are today. Right where you are, right how you are.
- The Lord handmade you, every single part of you - on purpose and with great delight.
- Your strength, sense of humor, emotional sensitivities, your unique gifts and talents, the shape of your body, the color of your hair, and the passion that burns like a fire in your chest for the things you care so much about- God made it all on purpose. God LIGHTS up when He thinks about you.
- He delights in who and where you are RIGHT NOW: not 20 pounds lighter, not with less issues or hurts, not as a better version of yourself. He thinks you are one of the best things He made, and when you love and celebrate yourself it honors Him, it brings Him glory as your Creator.
- God will always lead you to better: better places, deeper healing, and stronger truths. But you can't start from anywhere other than where you are right now. He does not despise your beginnings, nor should you.

QUESTIONS:

• Where are you at war with yourself?

• What are you working hardest to change about yourself? Why?

• Are there things you think you have to fix in order to be worthy, lovable, or safe? What is your list?

• Are you willing to give up the war with yourself? To rest? To listen instead of yell?

• Think about how you feel when you see someone that you adore: how your heart leaps out of your chest, how you can't help but smile, and how you need to be close to them as quickly as you can. Now, consider this: THAT is how God feels about you.

PART II

Self Care

CHAPTER 8
PLANT KILLER

"The Grass Is Greener Where You Water It."
- Neil Barringham

I have a confession to make - it's not pretty, admirable or brave - it's just the truth.

No matter how hard I try, I am a murderous plant killer.

I love my plants, but for the life of me, I cannot seem to keep them alive. My mother and grandmother both have green thumbs, but I have been known to kill even the hardiest of plants, and I live in the land of cactus. It's really almost a spiritual gift.

In an ironic twist, I absolutely *love* a gorgeous garden, or well manicured lawn, and especially any kind of flower. Seeing the life of lush landscapes feeds my soul in a way I can't explain. And yet, I am a serial plant killer.

When I left home for college at Texas A&M, someone obviously far more spiritual than me, gave me a *houseplant* as a graduation present. I am sure that it was intended to have a deeply spiritual meaning during my time at college, probably to serve as a living reminder to "water my soul daily" by reading my Bible and praying. But, y'all, that poor sucker never stood a chance.

At one point, a few months into our first semester, my roommate Holly heroically tried to save it, but it was too far gone. I had completely forgotten I even had a houseplant. And yet, even after it was completely dead, I still kept it on our back porch the entire year out of some kind of weird shame and guilt. Before I went home for the summer, I finally threw the whole thing out - basket, gift bow, rotting dried plant carcass and all, right into the dumpster.

I have tried again and again, but the best days of my poor plants' lives are the first days after I bring them home. They get potted in soil, watered, fertilized, and they stand in glory for a few weeks. Then without fail, I over-water or under-water them, and they die a slow, sad death.

I present them to the world proudly on my front porch in an attempt to say - "Look! I am growing and cultivating life and beautiful things! See what a good woman I am!" But in the end, they actually just stand as a neighborhood billboard revealing my ultimate failure at keeping things alive. (Listen, I know this does not bode well for my future children- but my hope is that they yell when they're hungry or thirsty, so it will force me to pay better attention.)

As an artist and musician, I travel a lot, and yes, it does affect my ability to daily care for something. But I'm afraid the principle here is telling no matter how you frame it.

I struggle to keep things alive that require consistency.

The truth is, I live in pendulum swings. When I am off the road and able to be at home, I eat right, work out, get plenty of sleep, invest in my friends and relationships, and generally take care of things. You know, *adulting*, like a boss.

And then, I'm on the road for days at a time on tour where the only nutrition available is the 24-hour Whataburger at 1:30 a.m. after a show. I never get enough sleep, and I cannot seem to execute a grammatically correct response to an email, much less stay on top of all of the things. I forget what city I am in or what day it is, and just walking up hotel stairs can make me winded for a good minute or two.

These two lifestyles could not be more opposite. I've lived this way since I was 16, and it has been an uphill-battle to learn to live differently: because let's be honest, it's not healthy, and it hardly helps me live to my fullest potential.

No matter how you shake it out: minimal care will never, ever bring out maximum potential.

It's the same principle as my sad, dead plants. Plants thrive and grow in a steady, nurturing environment. They will never grow to be as beautiful and strong as they could if they are starved or baked in the sun, and then occasionally drenched out of guilt a few times a year. It requires a very present and mindful person to cultivate and master a beautiful plant. I'm learning to be more present and mindful every day, but breaking old habits is not for the faint of heart.

I am really hard on myself. Terribly hard at times. I'm hard on my body, hard on my mind, and hard on my emotions. As a High Strung Woman I am strong - in some ways a "freak of nature" - but I know I can take it, so I push myself harder. But I've come to learn that is simply not a good way to live. It can be necessary in seasons, but I've learned that a lifetime filled with pushing too hard makes for a hard and lonely woman.

I have some big, crazy dreams. Dreams that demand the kind of sacrifice and work that could make a grown man cry. I can have my own issues believing God is for me and my dreams, so I work 10 times as hard to try and make them happen. I have pushed far beyond healthy limits into crazy places, and here is what I can tell you.

You cannot outwork God's plan for your life. What you can do is show up for your life, be faithful in all He has given you, and then you know what? You can rest in His promise that you *will* walk out all of the great things He has prepared for you. He's already done it, we just have to follow Him.

Learning to care for ourselves is perhaps the biggest priority of a High Strung Woman. We can't just wing it. My journey from push-yourself-as-hard-as-you-can-go to embracing the life-long path of learning what brings out the best in me hasn't been pretty, but it has drastically improved the quality of my life.

We're about to get into some really good stuff - things that can help you understand, manage, nurture, and care for how you are wired physically, emotionally, and physically. You deserve the very best care, my dear, for you are exceptional.

But first, dare to answer these questions.

QUESTIONS:

Take a deep breath, and don't be afraid of your answers- the truth sets us free remember? But when we keep trying to put makeup on our truths so they don't look so scary, girl - we don't get free. No judgement here- just observation.

• Where are you only giving yourself minimal care?

• Where do you struggle to feel like you are worthy of great care?

• Do you hold any beliefs about women who take time to care for themselves? What are they?

• Where are you outright neglecting your needs?

• What is one thing you can do today to start taking better care of YOU?

CHAPTER 9
I COME BY IT HONESTLY

After looking around, I realized that High Strung Women run in my family. They didn't all express it like I did, but I was absolutely not some genetic surprise. Chances are, they run in your family too.

So much of how we have tried to manage ourselves and navigate our worlds, we have learned by *example*. Our first example is our family, especially our Mamas, and the women we watched as young girls have had a profound effect on us.

The women that came before me were strong, fierce of spirit, and all pretty damn feisty in their own ways. One side of my family came from the church houses of Jackson, Mississippi, and the other from the saloons of Tulsa, Oklahoma. When my parents got married, a third generation Baptist preacher's son married the descendent of real life cowboys and train robbers. I mean, how could they not produce a wild-hearted rebel that also loves Jesus?

I inherited a lot of great things from this incredible lineage - a resilient spirit, fierce loyalty, deep faith and a never-give-up-attitude. But one of the things I did NOT inherit, was a real understanding of how to best care for myself emotionally, mentally, and in some ways - even physically. I don't mean knowing how to braid my hair or apply lipstick. I mean the kind of physical care that supports our mental and emotional health.

Make no mistake about it, as High Strung Women we require **tremendous** physical, emotional and mental care. Without it, we will struggle and we will suffer.

To be fair, this kind of emotional and personal self care

could easily have been considered superfluous and ridiculous in previous generations, where exhaustion and burnout were just considered a hazard of living. The women in my family were hearty survivors, and they obviously did their job well, as I am literally living proof.

But to survive, just means that it *didn't kill us*. Surviving is essential, but I reached a point in my life where I was looking for a whole lot more than just *not* dying. I was watching my aunts, cousins, and relatives hit major burnouts physically and emotionally. I was starting to experience some of that on my own as well, and I was not enjoying it. I could see where that path would lead me, but I couldn't shake the question "What if there was a different way, a better way?"

As I started to explore the idea of learning to do life differently, I came face to face with a harsh reality. I had a major attitude and deep judgement about women that practiced self care. At the time, I saw women that took time for themselves, did fun or fabulous things, or even just said "no" to requests as self indulgent and high maintenance. I couldn't think of two criticisms that I feared more. I had prided myself in burning myself up for the sake of others, relishing in the nobility of my sacrifice. But it was obvious that belief wasn't serving my health or my faith.

There are a lot of things that Christians get right, but I have to say- we are pretty bad at cultivating self love, especially among women. I was taught as a young girl that I should put myself last, always have a "servant's heart", and that my value was determined by how hard I worked. At the same time, I saw women older than me that I adored for their spunk and liveliness lose themselves in taking care of everyone else. I watched their radiance and beauty become shadowed by duty, sacrifice, and a life without a "No."

If I'm really honest, it looked a lot like martyrdom, and I started to hate it. I hated it for them, and I hated it for me.

I started to wonder *why* we as women always had to be the ones to sacrifice, to "die", so that *other* people didn't have to.

Our sacrifices made their lives easier, sometimes too easy from where I sat. Did we not deserve to have a good life too? How the hell did women become the token sacrifice?

My rebel heart hated it. But then my Christian guilt would kick in telling me I was just selfish, and I'd step back in line. It wasn't that I wasn't willing to sacrifice, or had to be first. I was really good at sacrificing myself, and had made it my life's anthem. But after years of it, I didn't feel noble or worthy. I felt low.

It was that there was something about it that just felt like.... suffering. Not the kind of suffering that's really hardship and produces endurance, but the kind of suffering that feels humiliating.

God doesn't humiliate us. He will lead us through hard times, and things that can feel like suffering at times- but a lifestyle of suffering was just not the heart of Jesus as I knew it.

I realized that it's a lie to believe that we as women always have to suffer, sacrifice or "die" so that others don't have to. It's a lie because Jesus already did that. He handled the sacrifice, so that we can LIVE. He handled the suffering so that we can be free.

Jesus calls us each to personal responsibility, and the first person we answer for is ourselves. You and I are held accountable for how we care for ourselves, as is everyone else. When we are over-extended, sacrificing ourselves completely to the needs of others- we are not reflecting Jesus, we are trying to replace Him. That's why we're so tired- it's not all ours to carry.

We'll get into this more in boundaries, but it is essential that every man, woman, and child face the full weight of their own life: their choices, their laundry, their homework, and their schedules.

A lifestyle of martyrdom is a surefire recipe for some worn out, resentful, frumpy, and angry women. How else should we feel when we've spent our lives denying ourselves, shushing our needs, and in every way communicating that we are the least important person in our world? If someone *else* did that to us, *we would HATE them.*

It was time to abandon the idea that being the martyr of my own life was noble. It was not.

It was undeniable that the women who dared to take time for themselves were healthier, happier, and just a hell of a lot more fun to be around. I mean, they glowed in a way that my skin hadn't seen in a decade. I was so attracted to this idea of life that it honestly scared me. How dare I choose myself?

But God hadn't called me to be a martyr, He had the sacrifices covered, and it was time to start showing up for myself.

I began to realize that holding onto my martyrdom had kept me from having to face the deep rooted beliefs that I didn't *deserve* to get to take care of myself. That I wasn't good enough to get to say no, to rest or to choose myself. I can weep all over again even just writing that out. Our enemy wants to keep us low and beaten up, but Jesus comes to heal our hearts and elevate us.

You, my sister, are so, so worthy of all of the time, care, and rest that you need. You don't have to earn it, apologize for it, or make up for it later. You get to say no. You get to say not now, you get to choose yourself. You are worthy, you hold inherent incredible value in the fact that God made you.

We must stop devaluing ourselves. You are not a second class citizen in God's family. You are high ranking royalty and a favorite of the King.

I don't know why it can feel so terrifying. I don't know why we as women are so much more comfortable dying a thousand deaths than living a big, good life. But I took a look around me and saw my future if I didn't learn to choose differently.

There IS a better way, and it is intentional, meaningful self care. Taking time for ourselves- to care for, repair, heal, and renew ourselves, only makes us, and those around us, better.

It's time to learn what taking care of ourselves looks like, and I think you're going to love it.

*"Self care is giving the world the best of you,
instead of what's left of you."*
-Katie Reed

QUESTIONS:

• What habits or standards did you learn from your family? What was valued in your childhood home?

• How have you viewed self care up to this point?

• Do you have any negative connotations with taking time for yourself?

• Where are you sacrificing yourself too much?

• Where are you DYING to be what you think you should be?

CHAPTER 10
GIRL, YOU ARE NOT A KIA.

"She remembered who she was,
and the game changed."
- Lalah Delia

L isten Sis. You and I have a world class engine inside of us. We have a luxury sports car super-engine that roars inside of our chest, and it does not take cheap gasoline. I'm talking Maserati, Ferrari, Aston Martin kind of car.

You are no bargain, entry-level Kia Rio sister girl, so we've got to stop treating ourselves like one.

We cannot keep feeding ourselves cheap gasoline, skipping oil changes, and trying to drive our sports car hearts like they are some beat up farm truck. We are not cheap, we are specialized and costly. We are not bargain-basement, discount women. We are exceptional, and we require *exceptional care.*

We *have got* to learn how to take better care of ourselves!

I know the car analogy may be a stretch, but let's put it in language we can all agree on here. You've got incredibly beautiful and sensitive feet (feet of the soul), and you can't keep putting those poor girls in cheap Payless high heels.

I have nothing against a good pair of cheap shoes, I love a bargain! But 3 hours in cheap high heels and you will pay for it in blood, pain, and tears.

I believe a great deal of our stress, anxiety, health issues, and even weight changes can be traced back to a lack of good self care. We simply haven't known how to take care of ourselves. But pull your chair up to the table Sis, cause we're about to learn.

WHEN WE CRASH

There have been times in my life when I legitimately felt like I could not go on, that I wasn't going to make it one more day. I'm not even being dramatic. I was physically exhausted, mentally drained and drowning emotionally. And each time, I crashed HARD.

I have experienced most of these deep points of exhaustion - these breaking points as a result of some kind of trauma. I'm not talking about a car wreck, kidnapping or abuse- I'm talking about things like breakups, disappointments, disagreements with family and friends, all the way to just life on a Tuesday. I am high-strung and extremely sensitive, and this makes all of my experiences "high definition."

Okay, so just to clarify that I am not being overly dramatic or ridiculous- let's focus on the real meaning of the word "trauma." Because there are very real and very deep experiences in this world of extreme traumas like rape, abuse, abandonment, war, death, loss and violence of all kinds, we usually reserve that word for the "big" experiences. I am not in any way trying to take away from those more serious experiences, but by reserving the attention and care *only* for the "big things", I think we are missing out on some really important insights. Let's start with the definition....

TRAUMA is defined as a deeply distressing or disturbing *experience.*

Trauma is defined by *what we experience*, not the details of what did or did not happen to us.

Our bodies have a very powerful response to trauma - both with big events and chronic, slower moving experiences like stress.

STRESS

One of the first indicators that I was a High Strung Woman dangerously careening on the edge of health and sanity, was that I.was.stressing. All day, every day.

I could turn the simplest task into an act of congress. I worried nonstop about how I said things and how they were interpreted by others. I lived in constant fear of doing something wrong.

My high-strung engine of a personality was killing me.

When you are a High Strung Woman and you don't understand or know how to care for yourself, you often end up in deep, chronic STRESS.

When you believe that everything about you is wrong, you are on guard 24-7 trying to keep yourself in line. Because you believe that you fundamentally cannot trust your natural instincts, you are always second guessing yourself.

This is *exhausting*. It is harder on your body than just about anything. In fact, stress opens the door to and feeds countless diseases in our bodies. Stress can shut down all non-essential functions so that the body basically goes into survival mode.

Sweet Moses, stress is the real deal. We know we need to stop being so stressed, but we don't know how.

Let's start with what stress really is.

According to stress.org:

"Stress is primarily a *physical response*. When **stressed**, the body thinks it is under attack and switches to 'fight or flight' mode, releasing a complex mix of hormones and chemicals such as adrenaline, cortisol and norepinephrine to prepare the body for physical action."

As I studied up on stress, I found this connection fascinating. There is a very clear and dramatic physical response to what goes on inside of us: in our thoughts and emotions- what we are thinking and believing. When we are chronically stressed, our bodies react like we are living in a constant state of danger.

This kind of stress is cancer to our bodies, and over time, it can turn toxic inside of us.

I experience my stress in many ways physically. But as I told y'all, I was used to being hard on my body - so I ignored it for far too long. If I'm honest, I did a great deal of damage. I was still wrapped up in the belief that being high maintenance was a bad thing - that the safest way to live was to require as little from the world as possible. But stress, like our emotions, will always find a way to express itself.

Here are just a few of my own personal physical responses to stress:

- I had chronic, and times debilitating shoulder and back pain. I carry a great deal of my tension in my shoulders. Over time I became a bundle of knots and was in a great deal of unnecessary pain. (I am honestly still working on this!)
- I would clench and grind my teeth both when I slept, and often when I was awake. This left me with TMJ, outrageously expensive dental work and a super sweet, extremely sexy mouthguard that I now have to wear every single night.
- I would so obsess over problems and challenges in my mind that they grew to be monstrous giants when they were really just hiccups. This took a toll on my marriage and other relationships.
- I worried constantly. My powerful imagination had me convinced at several different points that my loving, faithful husband was absolutely hiding a secret second family from me, or that we were all going to die on our flight to Kansas City. These are just a few of my best y'all. (Insert face palm emoji here)
- I had, and still do have, unbelievably stressful dreams. I cannot express the level of crazy my subconscious brain can go to in dreamworld, but suffice it to say, poor Ryan

has to say to me at least once a week, "Ab, you cannot be mad at me for what dream-Ryan did last night." To be fair, "Dream-Ryan," sounds like a stud - and real Ryan is. But unfortunately "Dream-Ryan" often acts out my greatest fears in my dreams. Real Ryan is *not* a fan of "Dream Ryan." (Yes, y'all can pray for him. Bless.)

• I often either can't sleep because my mind and body are buzzing with anxiety, or I can't stop sleeping because I am so exhausted. Sleep deprivation alone can make a woman crazy- it is used as a means of torture throughout history. Militants deprive prisoners of sleep to break down their will to live. Hello Mama's? In addition- sleeping too much **can** increase the risk of diabetes, heart disease, stroke and death according to several studies done over the years.

It's now easy to see that stress- the physical reaction to what is happening in our hearts and minds, is stunning in its power and unparalleled in its effect on our bodies.

As intimidating as fighting stress can seem, finding rest and peace does not have to be complicated. I have found great hope and help through some simple, but highly effective tools.

There's definitely not one "magic bullet" for beating stress, but as you study yourself and learn how you work, I know you will find the right combination for what you really need. It won't be the same for everyone, but these are some that have worked really well for me.

CALMING THE MIND

When I am spinning, and cannot seem to find solid ground, when I can't stop my thoughts, when I can't figure out exactly what I am feeling or why I am feeling that way, or when I am buzzing with anger... I will often use a guided meditation.

Meditations work wonders in several ways. They force you

to be still, calm your body, close your eyes and begin to slow your mind BY making you focus on something else, like your breath.

I will lay down, put a pillow over my eyes, and throw my headphones in as someone in a soothing voice talks me through slowing down my mind and relaxing my body. I am not overselling this when I say it has absolutely changed my life.

Becoming intentional about managing - not crushing or rejecting, but *guiding* what goes on inside of us in a healthy way is some grown woman work. But I believe it's essential for those of us who feel a great deal about everything. This is our first priority in learning self care as a high strung woman.

It is our responsibility to deal with what goes on inside of us. Make no mistake about it, we are accountable for how we take what goes on inside of us OUT on those OUTSIDE of us!

We must be as diligent to care for our insides as much as we are for our outsides.

Meditation is a great tool to slow us down and force us to pay attention to what is really going on inside of us. It allows us to pause the old go-to "tapes" of what's wrong, why it's wrong, or even how to deal with it. It forces us to stop, and *listen.*

Guided meditations are cheap (if not free on podcasts), available all the time and they are something you can do right away when you're starting to spin. It's a resource you can have ready any time, anywhere - providing some real relief from stress and anxiety. You can go sit in your car, hide in a bathroom stall at work, or even close your office door for 5 minutes. I've done them on airplanes during a bumpy flight that's scaring me to death, backstage before a big show, and multiple times during an extended family gathering like Christmas.

If you grew up in the church house like I did, you may have been taught that meditations were dangerous, new age B.S.

Like the practice of listening to someone help you slow your mind calm your body would wring the door wide open for the devil. Good grief.

The concept and practice of meditation is absolutely Biblical - the word alone is mentioned 23 times in the Bible. I have met Jesus in ways I never had before in that calm, focused space of being present in my body and mind. I don't close my eyes and slow my breaths to meet someone there I don't know. I do those things to be reminded of the Truth. When I remember how big my God is and how He cares for me, I feel better immediately.

(At some point I do want to create and produce meditations specifically for High Strung Women, so stay tuned!)

QUESTIONS

• Where is your high strung personality killing you?

• Where is your body trying to tell you you're stressed?

• Do you crash hard? What usually leads you up to this point? Get specific- you'll learn some things!

CHAPTER 11
WORK IT (OUT)

I have learned that some days there is nothing better for a High Strung Woman than a good workout. If you break the word down, it is literally a means to "work it out." And when you have a lot of feelings, thoughts and tension, you need a means to work through it physically.

Earlier we said that when we are *stressed,* our bodies think we are under attack and switch to 'fight or flight' mode. This releases a complex mix of hormones and chemicals into our bloodstream *to prepare our body for **physical action***.

Back in the caveman days when our greatest enemy wasn't swimsuit season, but actual terrifying beasts that wanted to eat us for dinner, stress and adrenaline served a very important role in keeping us ALIVE.

When faced with danger, our brains told our bodies to release all the energy resources we have to help us RUN away from the lion trying to eat us. Because you know, survival.

Today, we no longer live in a constant state of fear from things that want to eat us for dinner, but our body's response to danger and stress has not changed. But how our minds classify "danger" has changed.

Think about it. How many times a day are you like "Oh NOOOO."

Things like- "I didn't remember to send that email. I don't have enough time to get this done. I forgot Sam's school lunch at home. We have to sell our house and move in 2 months- how is that going to happen? I'm embarrassed of my body and feel like I need to crash diet. Why isn't she responding to my text? What have I done to make her mad?"

Sis, that's nothing but stress - and a LOT of it.

Stress is not something new. It's been around as long as people have. So why is it killing us now?

Our bodies are reacting to stress the same way they always have, but we are not responding to that rush of hormones like we used to. Our bodies still send the same rush of chemicals and hormones to give us the burst of energy we needed to run away from danger, and yet we are sitting in cubicles, carpool lines, and in our living rooms. We aren't using that energy to run away from danger, we are sitting *in it*: wave after wave after wave.

Today we experience stress all day, every day, which results in the same flood of hormones and chemicals as when we saw the lion about to pounce on us back in the day - but with NO physical release.

We are drowning in our own body's reactions to danger, and because it's not being worked out, it turns toxic inside our bodies and causes major problems.

This is incredibly important to know and understand. Everyone has stress, but in my opinion, High Strung Women experience a greater deal of stress than most people.

We feel all of the things all the time. We have more going on inside of us at any given moment, and because of the sheer volume of what we are processing and trying to survive, we are stressing.

Stress is expressed in our bodies, so to help our minds and our bodies effectively deal with the effects of stress, we must work it out physically. We have to move, sweat and challenge our bodies so they can process the flood of hormones and chemicals they've been filled with all day. When we are stressed and not moving our body, we feel it. It's just a matter of time before it starts to do some damage.

There are lots of great options for exercise, movement, and working it out physically- but I'm going to talk about the 2 that have really helped me.

WE CAN PICK UP HEAVY THINGS

First of all: Girl - you're gonna need some resistance training.

I know, I know. Our lives feel like one giant, unending session of resistance training with a red-faced, mean, Jillian Michaels-lady yelling at us. But hear me out.

You don't just need a little walk around the block. There are days when we need to sweat like we mean it, like we need it. Because Sis, we DO need it.

Before you go all crazy on me, here's what I mean. I'm not talking about working out to lose weight or change your body. I'm talking about working out to clear your mind, find your sanity and sweat out the stress hormones. We work out to remind ourselves that we're strong and we're not stuck.

Working out is something no one else can do for us. It's not something we can buy. It's something we do for us. It's inherently self serving, and self healing. In my opinion, it is absolutely essential for a High Strung Woman. I do not function well without it. My husband and family can vouch for this.

Here are a few tips I have learned:
- Start with a workout at HOME that focuses on building strength. There are tons of apps, Youtube videos, and health programs. They will typically utilize weights or resistance bands. I started with a set of 5 lb. dumbbells and worked from there.
- You do NOT have to do the hardest workout in the world. Hard work can be done, and I mean it, with a set of 3 lb. dumbbells. Our goal here is working out stress and strengthening our bodies, not punishing them.
- Working out at home enables you to PAUSE the damn workout when you need to. To this day, if I am struggling through a workout, I will pause it - get some water or

walk it out around my house. Hell, I have even had a snack in the middle of a workout when I was hangry. No shame here!

- Go at your own pace. I took a 90 day program with 3 sections and did the first 2 sections for 9 months before I felt ready to tackle the last one. Did you know you can do that? Hah! Yes you can! You are in charge of you and of listening to your body- if their pace is too fast, too hard, then take over!

- I have found the most success in doing a workout that I enjoy, and want to come back to. What I mean is, if it feels like torture and you hate every minute of it, you are NOT going to want to come back. And, as I am sure you have experienced, what we really want to do is what always wins out!

- Start with just 1 day a week of resistance training and work your way up. My body can't handle much more than 3 days a week of weights, so I walk the other days or rest.

- Most programs are built for maximum results in the shortest time frame. That's fine- but if you find that your workout is STRESSING you out because it's too intense- you are now working against what we are trying to do. Lower your weights, pause to catch your breath, or only use half of the workouts for the week. On the other days, you can walk, do yoga or just rest!

- Crank up some music that gets you fired up and prepare to feel like a badass! I enjoy dancing, although it's not pretty, or singing along between sets with weights. This is another benefit of working out from home, although it can be done at Planet Fitness if you're prepared to go viral!

I love the way strength training allows me to push back on what is pushing on me. When done right, and at your own pace- I think you'll find you love it too!

When we've got a lot going on, we HAVE to have some place to work it out, and not just mentally, emotionally, or spiritually. Sweat does great things for the body and the soul. Moving your body is incredibly important for a strong mindset, and it is vital to process all those stress hormones.

Good things come to those who sweat.

THE YOGAS

During my first round of counseling with my therapist Wendy, she kept "encouraging" (rather firmly) that I try Yoga.

I was super annoyed at the idea. I felt I had to be chasing something, pushing something or running from something to feel motivated to exercise. The idea of stretching just seemed like a waste of time. (You can see now why I was a bundle of muscle knots and tension, right?)

I can remember looking at her and saying "What's the deal? Why does everyone keep telling me to try Yoga? Do I not seem chill?" It was a joke. But obviously not a good one.

My girl Allison loves her some hot yoga, and she would rave about how good she felt after a class. But I just couldn't handle the thought of a hot, humid room with strangers. I already lived in Texas, and it was hot enough. Plus, I don't like strangers! I mean, if I'm honest, I don't like anyone when I'm hot and sweaty.

But after my back and shoulder tension got so bad that I was in constant pain, I thought maybe I could become of those lean, zen girls after all... like Jennifer Anniston. Let's be honest, anything that gets us closer to Rachel's arms c. 1999 is worth a try, am I right?

Because I generally loathe group exercise, I found a Rodney Yee yoga set of workouts I could do at home. As you might imagine, I was annoyed and frustrated most of the first few sessions. But after struggling through holding weird poses for what felt like an eternity, I finally laid down in the last pose, my personal favorite, relaxation pose. I was shocked.

I didn't feel done, exhausted, or spent. Somehow my body felt renewed, and rested.

As I kept coming back, I got better at getting out of my head and into my body, and I realized how closely meditations and yoga were connected. That combination is powerful when you have a storm raging inside of you and can't find your feet.

I'll never forget the day I laid down for relaxation pose at the end of a session and I was overwhelmed with a sense of grief I had apparently been avoiding. I knew I was feeling blue, but as my body finally relaxed, so did my emotions. They at last flowed like they should. Laying on my yoga mat I cried.

In that moment I was overwhelmed with gratitude to my body for telling me what was wrong. I didn't know I needed to cry, I hadn't let myself tune in. Our bodies hold so much insight for us, but we won't hear what they are saying if we don't ever stop to listen.

Rejecting the belief that we are a non-stop self improvement project, and instead embracing who we are and where we are right now is honestly, pretty radical.

In today's world of the glorification of busy, stressed and exhausted women we must be willing to be misunderstood by others, in order to better understand ourselves.

Why? Why does all of this matter so much? I think Melody Beattie says it best in her book "The Language Of Letting Go":

> "Self care means learning to love the person we're responsible for taking care of - ourselves.
> We do not do this to hibernate in a cocoon of isolation and self indulgence; we do it so we can better love others, and learn to let them love us.
> SELF CARE ISN'T SELFISH; IT'S SELF ESTEEM."
> - Melody Beattie

QUESTIONS

• Are you moving your body enough to process your stress?

• Where are some creative places of your day you can incorporate meditations and movement?

• Where is your body trying to tell you something is wrong? What hurts?

CHAPTER 12
SELF CARE HOTLIST

"Nurtured, nourished people who love and care for
themselves are the delight of the universe.
They are well-timed, efficient and divinely led."
-Melody Beattie

Since we now know that minimal care will never bring out maximum potential, we must be willing to take a good look at how we are taking care of ourselves. A lifestyle of neglecting, punishing and pushing ourselves does not serve us or those we love.

It's time to show up for ourselves by paying attention to what our minds and bodies really need so we can bring the best of ourselves to this one life we have been given. We are strong, but we are also sensitive. Learning to take great care of ourselves may sound intimidating or overwhelming at first, but I've found that it comes down to some rather simple, but important things. By simply becoming aware of how the following factors deeply affect your mental, physical and emotional state, you will be well on your way to major improvements in self care.

"SLEEP IS THE BEST MEDITATION."
-Dalai Lama

Oh girl, you need your sleep. Like for real. Rest is a huge part of self care for a High Strung Woman.

There are days when you need your sleep more than your

workout, your perfectly balanced meal, or to get it all done. Sleep is one of the best things you can do for yourself. It's when our bodies repair things, relax, reset and HEAL. If you're not getting enough sleep - and I mean full-on REM cycle sleep, you are headed straight for a major crash.

> *"The way you feel while you're awake depends in part on what happens while you're sleeping."*
> -National Heart, Blood, and Lung Institute

If you're not feeling good or struggling through your days, a good place to start is to evaluate the quality of your sleep.

If you have a hard time sleeping well, here are some things I've found helpful:

- Have a clear bedtime ritual. I watch my sister Kate, the Supermom, do this with my nephews every single night: bath time, lotion, clean pajamas, brush teeth, lavender oil, story time, lights out and close the door. The entire process is telling their little minds and bodies it's time for bed. It's time to rest, sleep and turn off.

- My night-time ritual has coincided with my new-found love for beauty practices at home. I used to be terrible about washing my makeup off, much less putting on a moisturizer. I would fall into bed exhausted and chaotic. I now love my nighttime routine. I take a shower, put on clean pajamas, brush my teeth, and apply my skincare routine. I head to my bedroom where I'll have some essential oils diffusing, turn out all the lights and do a sleep meditation with my headphones in (which is also helpful for drowning out snoring husbands). *It is glorious.* I am clean, everything smells good, it's dark, I'm snuggled under covers and I welcome in that sacred time of sleep.

- I don't have kids yet, and I know it can be a million times harder, but prioritizing your sleep is a good and healthy boundary for your kids to understand as much as you can do it. *Sleep is important*, and it's especially important for Mommy.

- Don't scroll through your phone in bed. The light signals to your brain it should be awake, and as a result won't wind down for sleep easily.
- Try using a smell like a lotion, or an essential oil that you only use when it's time to sleep. Smelling that every night will start an association in your brain that it's time to wind down. (For me, it's lavender and cedar wood.)
- Sleep in a dark, cold room, with a low relaxing noise like a ceiling fan.
- Some people really find deeper rest when they use things like earplugs and face masks. I am a big fan, as my husband snores like an Alaskan Brown Bear with a cold.
- If you need extra help going to sleep you can try melatonin, Olly "Sleep" gummies, lavender, magnesium, blackout curtains or even a sound machine.
- Now, I don't know that there is a magic amount of sleep that's the same for every person. I have seen the recommended amount range from 6-to-10 hours for an adult. That's a pretty big range. I know some people who are energized for a full 20-hour day after just four hours. I am *not* one of those people, but as always, listen to your body. If you need more sleep, Real Housewives can wait until the weekend to be watched. I promise, you'll feel much better from more sleep, and you'll probably be less likely to throw a drink in someone's face at work the next day. Hah!

BEAUTY SLEEP BONUS: Want some proof that good sleep changes everything? Two of Jennifer Lopez's self proclaimed beauty secrets are that she gets a lot of sleep and drinks a ton of water. Now listen, I don't know what unicorn blood J L0 drinks, but, good grief if she doesn't look better at 50 than she did at 23. She has 10-year-old twins, (and I'm sure like, 3 nannies) all of the dollars to do "beauty treatments," surgeries or whatever else she is doing. All I know is that I look like something from the Zombie apocalypse when I have to stay up all night, but I can look like a new woman after a full night of sleep. This girl is gonna err on the side of more sleep as best I can.

"YOU GOTTA LET ME NAP, OR I'M GONNA GET CRANKY!"
-Joey From FRIENDS

If you can't get a full night of sleep because you have kids, a husband that snores, or noisy neighbors, let me introduce you to my best friend - naps.

I *love* naps, maybe even too much. I love them because it feels like a quick reset for my mind, body and day. On days when I am especially emotionally strung out, and can't seem to get over the hurdle with meditations or anything else, I will straight up just go back to sleep and try again. And you know what? *I always feel better.*

Some people hate naps, but I find them to be like a midday renewal when I am dragging. If you can fit one in - in your car, at your desk, on the floor of your classroom, or even while your kids are watching another episode of PJ Masks - Sis, do it. Even if you don't go all the way to sleep, you are resting your body and your mind which lowers stress. When we lower stress and get ourselves out of a "danger" state, we are able to make better decisions, have more grace and be kinder both to ourselves and others.

HYDRATE

We will never get even close to our best if we are dehydrated.

Everything in your life gets better when you drink more water. It's simple and far from a glamorous new life hack. But we can eat the best food, workout every single day and still live in major physical distress if we are not getting enough water.

Did you know that some of the signs that you are not drinking enough water include: fatigue, headaches, grumpiness, lowered mental clarity and muscle tension? Oh, and let's not forget that we often eat more when our bodies are really just thirsty.

I really struggled with drinking enough water until I bought a big water bottle that I now keep with me all day. Drinking enough water makes a huge difference in how my body feels, how my face looks, and how clear I am on whether or not I am hungry, tired, or thirsty. It's really easy to mix those three things up and if you're default is to eat when you feel bad, which is mine, you can find yourself in a bad way when you just don't have to be.

You can do your own research on how much water is enough for you, but I carry a large water bottle and just refill it several times a day. (As always, take the time to sit still and *listen* to your body before you starve it, stuff it, numb it or move it.) Your body will tell you the truth. We'd be a lot farther along in life if we just listened to ourselves and honored what we heard.

BONUS: Drinking a ton of water is one of the best things you can do for your complexion and skin. Hydration makes your face look less haggard, dry and wrinkly. Drinking Diet Coke is not so good for your complexion, or so I have been told.

DON'T BE HANGRY

This is a place where I pushed my body really hard and paid for it in big ways. For example: I am totally one of those people who get "HANGRY," meaning, I can get full-on angry when I'm hungry. Put those two things together, and you get the word and state of "hangry." It's really not pretty, and it can be flat-out dangerous for anyone around me. I am so well known for it, that one Christmas, my brother gave me a small fanny-pack filled with granola bars. Puzzled, I looked at him, and he said, "Some people need EpiPens ready for emergencies. You need snacks." Hah!

So, I have to start by making sure I feed myself. That sounds like I am some waif wasting away because I forget to eat. Um, no. I never *forget* to eat, and I am far from wasting away. But I can get so focused and obsessed with getting something done, that I can look up hours later and already be in what Ryan and I call "the dark place." It's a bad place to be, and my marriage has suffered severely there more than once. "The dark place" is when you have passed the normal threshold of hunger and become crazed, panicked and angry. It's even worse than just "hangry," and it should be avoided at all costs. (I try to remember that I'll never get so much done that it is worth crashing and burning in the dark place.) Don't be crazy, Sis. Stop and feed yourself.

Bonus: When we don't prioritize feeding ourselves we end up binging, overeating, or eating tons of trash food far more as we try to swing back from the dark place. Desperation breeds bad decisions. But when we DO prioritize it we make much better decisions and experience more physical stability to go about our day. Don't be a mad hangry martyr Sis- feed yourself.

WHAT'S ON YOUR PLATE?

Whether you are stuffing yourself, starving yourself, or just eating low quality foods - this is the fuel we are putting in our high power performance engine. Low quality fuel is really hard on our engines, and it can lead to major breakdowns both physically and emotionally.

There's enough diet and nutrition literature out there to wrap our globe, and I feel like I've read and tried at least half of it, but here are my highlights:

1. Whole, unprocessed foods go a long way in providing high quality nutrition to your body, mind and soul. Eat

real food as your fuel and you are on your way to an engine with fewer breakdowns.

2. You cannot underfeed (fuel) nor overfeed (fuel) your body and expect it to perform at a high level. If you starve yourself, your body will shut things down, because it's just trying to survive. If you stuff yourself, you will be lethargic, sleepy and in some kind of physical distress. Pay attention to your body, and eat good food when you are hungry.

3. When you're not hungry and you want to eat, figure out what you're feeling, wanting to hide from or avoiding. Geneen Roth has several fantastic books on this topic, including *Women, Food, and God.* I believe that as women we use food as more of a coping mechanism, numbing agent and hiding place than any drug, drink or high in this world. But food is intended to be our fuel to live our lives. And when we're using it for anything else, we need to pay attention to what's really going on.

You can't live off of Chick-fil-A, Lean Cuisine pizzas and bags of Doritos and Diet Coke forever. I mean, technically, you can *live* on it, but it won't be pretty or for very long. Believe me, I've tried.

After most of my life believing otherwise, I now see that it's ridiculous to say that you're too busy to eat good food. Eating good food only enables us to do more, better. We pay now or we pay later, but Sis, we *always* pay and see the return on what we've fed ourselves. If your body is crying out to you - in terms of rashes, digestive upset, sleep issues, pain, tension or foggy brain - LISTEN UP! Two of the first places we can start to pay attention and make better choices are with the food we eat, and how much water we're drinking.

In my experience blacklisting things, including some foods, in our lives only creates more stress. Because life never goes perfectly according to plan. But making a conscious effort to eat real, good food when you're hungry is what we're talking about here. This is about saying that you matter - you are worthy of good, high quality food.

A question that Geneen Roth uses a lot in her work is "What kind of life are you living when you look at your plate?"

When you look down at your plate what do you see?

- Is it sad and restrictive? Based in fear of food, fear of your body and the need to control?
- Is it excessive and serving as a stand-in for the flavor and abundance you really want out of life and you can't seem to find? Are you using food to cope with your stress?
- Is it so random and at the mercy of everything and everyone else that you have no idea when or what your next meal will be?

Sis, any of these are not healthy. They are not good for you, and it's time to show up for your life by feeding yourself good, high quality fuel. You've got big things to do, and gas station snacks will not sustain you on your climb of Everest.

Eat like it's what keeps you alive - because it *is* what keeps you alive.

SUNSHINE MAKES YOU HAPPY

Did you know that vitamin D deficiency is considered an *epidemic* in the United States?

Over 40 percent of the U.S. population has less than optimal amounts of vitamin D, and it has a major impact in our mood, health and immune system. When sunshine hits our skin, our body responds by producing vitamin D.

When I told my doctor I hadn't been feeling great (brain fog, weight and mood), she tested my vitamin D levels and found them low. She prescribed a supplement and 10 minutes a day of sunshine with no sunscreen.

Sunshine goes hand-in-hand with fresh air. It's good for our bodies and our souls. No matter the weather, make a point to get outside for a while every single day. Get your kids outside, take the dog on a walk, do yard work with your husband, eat lunch outside or perhaps engage in my all time favorite serotonin-boosting, happy-inducing power activity: drinking margaritas on a patio with your girlfriends.

LAUGHTER

"Laughter is a sunbeam of the soul."

-Thomas Mann

In a world that takes itself far too seriously, laughter has become dangerously underrated. But laughter is incredibly important in our lives. Isn't it strange how we often don't realize how much we've missed it until we are wiping the happy tears from our eyes and catching our breath from laughing so hard?

We must learn to seek out, welcome and fully embrace laughter in our lives. Medically and scientifically speaking, laughter has an incredible effect on our bodies, and is a great tool in dealing with stress.

Laughter not only decreases stress hormones, but it triggers the release of endorphins, our happy hormones. Endorphins are what make us feel *good*- so we need all of those we can get.

According to the Mayo Clinic, laughter relieves stress, soothes tension (both physically and relationally), improves your immune system, relieves pain, helps with depression, and improves your mood. Being able to find humor in even the hardest and most challenging circumstances just makes for a happier life. In addition, when you can find humor in a tough situation, you can also likely find a new angle to solve the problem! Laughter relaxes us, and often helps us loosen our grip on the very things that we've been afraid of.

I personally find that some of my best laughs occur at times when I should "not" be laughing. My Mimi, Jane Walker (the

Southern Baptist Matriarch), calls it the "church giggles." This name comes from years of sitting through serious church services, working very hard to behave yourself, and yet losing all composure when you see something wickedly funny in a place where you should not be laughing.

Examples can include, but are not limited to: a church soloist singing with her heart out but not hitting a single note, someone passed out asleep during church with their mouth wide open, or an overly dramatic worship dancer who has decided the church sanctuary is their Broadway. All of these things are only made funnier by the cultural expectation that you should "*not*" be laughing.

These are the church giggles: dying of laughter inside, desperately looking away, fighting to keep silent, shoulders shaking, holding your breath, and tears rolling down your cheeks. Look, my best advice to you at this point is to pretend that you are overcome with emotion by the service, bow your head and upper body to "pray", and hope that those around you buy in. Perhaps even lay their own hands on your back in support to really sell it.

I have come to believe that these outbursts of "inappropriate laughter" are your body's way of saying- "Stop being so damn serious and hard on yourself all the time!" There are times when we just *need* to laugh!

So girl, let yourself laugh. Quit watching so much drama and find you a show that makes you belly laugh. Your mind and body will thank you!!!

"Self-care is how you take your power back."
– Lalah Deli

QUESTIONS

• What is the biggest need in your self-care list? What steps can you take TODAY to make changes?

• What is NOT working with the way you have been caring for yourself?

• Go through each of these sections and give yourself a score from 1-10 to rate your current level of self care!

PART III
Boundaries

CHAPTER 13
YELLOWSTONE

Yellowstone National Park is one of the most magical, breathtaking, wild and dangerous parts of the world, and I'll never forget the first time I saw her.

I was an annoyed teenager on our first family vacation to Montana, preoccupied with missing my friends back home. We woke before dawn and drove about an hour in the dark to the big park entrance in West Yellowstone. Like any impatient teenager, I expected to see something noteworthy as soon as we passed through the gate: Yogi Bear waving at us, perhaps a friendly moose standing in a pond or at least a waterfall. After 20 minutes of driving in the dark woods, I was convinced this whole national park thing was a scam, or at best, a snooze-fest.

Crowded in the backseat with my adolescent siblings, arguing over who had more room, we finally rounded a bend on that dark two-lane road, and the universe split wide open.

In an instant, we were swept out of the forest and into a brilliant mountain valley drenched in early morning sunlight. Steam rolled off the sparkling Yellowstone River as a large herd of elk crossed the water calling to each other. Bright wildflowers covered the river banks, tree-covered mountains surrounded us, and the smell of a forest full of pines was invigorating.

I swear my heart stopped when I saw it all. It was the most magical thing I had ever seen in my sassy 15 years of life. What an introduction to the concept of National Parks for a punk-faced teenager from Texas! I was in awe of this magical place. A place of wonder, a treasure our government *fiercely protects* from development, poachers, and misuse. This was no scam, and definitely no snooze. This was *incredible*.

Surely, this was a very special place. Surely, this was some kind of *sacred ground*.

As someone who sees and hears God through nature, this beautiful, wild place stirred my very soul. The God I experienced in nature was so much bigger and closer than the God I heard about in church. Here herds of bison roamed the hills, fuzzy long-legged elk calves wobbled beside their mothers eating grass by the streams, geysers shot into the air, and roaring waterfalls trembled the ground on which we stood to observe them. It was wide-open wonder.

As we continued on our journey through the park, I noticed another aspect of Yellowstone. Our trip was at the peak of summer visitor season, when people travel from all over the world to catch a glimpse of its beauty. There were more buses than I could count at rest stops, masses of people swarming up to see Old Faithful, and oh, the traffic on those two-lane winding roads.

My dad is an avid outdoorsman, and he raised all three of us to have deep respect and appreciation for the code of life in the wild. One hour in Yellowstone will prove that there are a lot of people who were not raised that way.

Watching tourists stumble out of their cars in their flip flops and tank tops across the mountain prairie to try and take a picture with a 2,000-pound buffalo like he was Mickey Mouse, left my family in open-mouthed shock.

Buffalo are wild, dangerous animals. They fight every single day to stay alive and not be eaten by other wild and dangerous animals. They are not cows. They are not domestic pets. When they feel threatened, or even when they just feel like it, they can throw you 20 feet into the air, harpoon you with their horns or trample you (likely in front of a crowd with cameras). It's a brutal way to go viral, but if you Google it, you'll see!

Park rangers work long hours to ensure the safety of well meaning but clueless park tourists. If you ask them, I would venture to say that most of them didn't get into the park service to protect tourists, but to protect the beauty and wonder of the land and animals that live in our National Parks.

The park rangers know that if you stay within the *proper boundaries* that respect wild animal's space, you not only preserve its beauty, but you get to see and experience some truly incredible things.

Things like bull elk bugling and fighting in the fall, bison calves running and playing on the prairie, a wolf pack crossing the valley in a dead run on the hunt, the force of a geyser at sunset, baby black bears rolling in wildflowers, or perhaps even a 600 pound Grizzly Bear tearing up and eating his dinner on the banks of a river. But you cross the boundary on any of those sights, and you are in immediate danger. It's not about fear, it's about respect.

Without the strict enforcement of the boundaries, rules and respect that both the land and animals of Yellowstone deserve, I have no doubt that there would be widespread damage to it's beauty by now. I'm not saying people would do it because they are bad, I'm just saying it would be a natural consequence of so much unmanaged human traffic in the area.

In order to protect what we hold valuable, we must build boundaries to respect and care for it. There must also be consequences when boundaries are broken.

Not only can you go to jail for major offenses in Yellowstone, you actually fall under federal jurisdiction. That may sound like overkill to you, but I believe it's absolutely necessary. Something this valuable must have strong boundaries with significant consequences.

We cannot allow precious things to be trashed, used up or violated simply because people don't know better. We must learn to teach them how to respect them, and care for them. And as always, we must start with ourselves.

QUESTIONS:

• Do you find it difficult to know what's yours to take care of and what's not?

• Do you take better care of other people than yourself?

• What is sacred in your life?

• What are some things you want to start treating like they are sacred?

We can't teach others to respect that which we don't respect ourselves.

CHAPTER 14
"MINE."

When I was three years old, my parents bought me a bright green, Fisher-Price turtle-shaped sandbox. If you're a child of the 80s, you know the one. I thought it was the most glorious thing in the world, because for the very first time, I was told that it was "mine." Mine is a *very* important word for a three year old, and the power of the idea of having something of my very own was unlike anything I had ever known. It lit me up inside, and it still does.

A few weeks later, my Dad and I were in the midst of an important toddler life-lesson entitled, "Who's The Boss?" As you might imagine, he felt I needed some instruction in this area.

I found myself on the receiving end of a very serious lecture on why HE was, in fact, THE boss. I heard him out, sighed loudly, and then with all of the seriousness and sincerity in my little 3-year-old body looked him square in the eye and said, "But I'm the boss of my *own sandbox*, right Dad?"

My poor Father's eyes widened as he chuckled and realized what exactly he was in for in raising this strong-willed daughter of his. While he buckled in for the parenting ride of his life, I found a very important truth as a spirited little person - *I very, very much needed a protected place to call my own.*

At the time, it was as simple as being able to retreat to and just sit in my sandbox when my world wasn't as I wanted. That little green sandbox got me through many-a-hard time as a kid, but as I got older, I realized it was really a physical example of my need for boundaries, both from the outside world as well as *on* my big personality.

We talked previously about the profound impact a master can have on the force and effect of a fire by using limits to harness the fire's strength. These limits also serve to *protect the fire from destroying itself.* Without these limits, the fire would burn itself out fast and hard. It's life and effect would be limited to a flash.

Think about that for a second. Without healthy and appropriate limits, the glory of who God has made you to be could burn out and be limited to a flash. We're not here to burn ourselves up. We are here to *shine,* sis. To shine long and bright every single day that the Lord gives us on this Earth.

Working to know our limits, build healthy boundaries and stand our sacred ground is some of the most important work you will do to care for yourself as a High Strung Woman. I won't kid you here, this kind of work is not for sissies. But it is a battle worth fighting every single day.

We are living in a time in history where women are pushing for more - equal pay, justice, and an end to sexual abuse and harassment. We're breaking through glass ceilings that male-dominated institutions have held over our heads for generations. It is exciting, and yet it can feel like the wild west at times, with a shootout just around every corner. It takes an incredible amount of courage to fight for any of these things. We are trying to figure out what rules to break and what boundaries to build. It can be extremely confusing, and my heart aches as I watch women swing between bravery in the right places and anger and chaos in others. It is messy, but absolutely necessary to keep showing up and working it out.

But I am not talking about limits, boundaries or rules that *others* have put on us, our careers, our dreams, or our bodies. I am talking about *our* internal boundaries, our "in-house security system" which is vital for us to keep safe what we hold precious.

In this place, limits and boundaries are not about holding

you back, crashing into a ceiling, or being controlled by others. Boundaries are actually the essence of taking good care of yourself, showing up for yourself, saying "I matter."

"Daring to set boundaries is about having the courage to love ourselves, even when we risk disappointing others."
-Brené Brown

As we start to pay more attention to where we thrive and feel safe, and to where we feel threatened and chaotic, we begin to discover our core boundaries. As we figure out what our job is and what it isn't, we are freed up in a way that changes everything.

It all starts by choosing to really *learn* about rather than judge ourselves. We have been professional critics, but we need to become master observers. We must start from a place of observation and radical acceptance. Let yourself be exactly where you are today. Let yourself feel your feelings.

What does your heart feel? Pain? Hope? Disappointment?

Let your body tell you how it feels: Tired? Punished? Neglected? Unchallenged? In pain?

Stop passing judgement or trying to change anything. Just dare to *listen*. We have abandoned the war and are learning to work WITH ourselves as partners, not fighting ourselves like enemies.

The more that we learn about our true selves, not who we think we need to be for others, or what is expected of us- we begin to see the lines of what define our sacred ground. The lines that we draw physically, emotionally, spiritually, financially, and mentally that surround, that will protect our sweet spot- where we operate in health and strength, where we know rest, and where we honor ourselves and our Creator by living our best lives.

> **"Walls keep everybody out.**
> **Boundaries teach people where the door is."**
> **-Mark Groves**

At the most basic level, a boundary is a line that divides, a marker that separates. In terms of property boundaries define ownership. You can do what you want on land you own, but on land you don't own, you cannot. We are held responsible for what happens on our property. However, we cannot control, nor will we be held accountable for, what happens on someone else's land.

Dr. Henry Cloud and Dr. John Townsend are the leading authorities on this topic, and they have written several incredible books on boundaries. I recommend them ALL, and if they had an endorsement deal, this girl would be trying to sign with them. Their teachings and insights changed.my.life. I'm not kidding, these truths drastically altered my marriage, my relationships with family, work, and friends. I read and re-read their books on the regular, because as a recovering people pleaser, I need these truths on an IV drip straight to my veins.

Cloud and Townsend define a boundary as "a personal property line that marks those things for which we are responsible. Boundaries define who we are, and who are not."

They break boundaries down into four key areas:
- **"Physical boundaries** help us determine who may touch us and under what circumstances.
- **Mental boundaries** give us the freedom to have our own thoughts and opinions.
- **Emotional boundaries** help us to deal with our own emotions and disengage from the harmful, manipulative emotions of others.
- **Spiritual boundaries** help us to distinguish God's will from our own and give us renewed awe for our Creator."

I grew up in a world where under the banner of

"Christianity"- obeying Jesus and serving others - there were very few boundaries especially when it came to people.

Don't get me wrong, there were hard and fast limits on profanity, adultery, disobedience and all other things considered "sin." Those boundaries were rock solid, even legalistic at points. But when it came to the daily, real-life relationships with others - especially within the church - I struggled deeply.

We literally never said "no" to people. We weren't *allowed* to say "no" to people. It was considered unkind, ungracious and ungrateful. Even as a child, I was expected to let people hug me, say pretty much anything to me, and I was expected to always have a smile on my face. Preacher's kids weren't allowed to have bad days, dislike someone, or just be "over it."

But the beauty of childhood is that there is only so much you can control in a kid. Eventually, their truth is going to bust out. And no matter how uncomfortable it may be for the adults, their honesty can't be contained.

I'll never forget the Sunday I had had enough. I straight up RAN from an old lady at church. I mean it. I ran from her like I got the Holy Ghost at pentecostal church camp.

I didn't run because she was a mean old lady. She wore fabulous hats that matched her fancy Sunday church suits and wrote me the sweetest birthday cards every single year. But she was also notorious for hugging me way too hard, pinching my cheeks until they stung, and hanging onto me for far longer than I was comfortable.

So one Sunday after the service, I heard her call my name and start hobbling straight for me. I don't know what it was that lit my normally well behaved tail end on fire that day, but apparently I had just had enough. It was like my body knew it before my brain did. I caught her eye and fled that sanctuary like my Sunday church dress was on FIRE. I sprinted down the hallway in my clinking patent-leather church shoes to the farthest possible bathroom, and scrambled into a stall to hide.

Why? Why would I run from a geriatric church lady?

Well, she said things to me I didn't like, pinched my cheeks too hard, and she always smelled like mothballs. To sum it up: *I just didn't like it*. And on that Sunday, it was enough to make me run the church forty.

Breathless from my sprint, standing on the toilet in the bathroom stall so she couldn't see my feet, I was sure I had left her in the dust. But as I let out a sigh of relief, I heard the creak of the bathroom door, shuffling feet, and then a wall of scent hit my nostrils. Mothballs.

Oh HELL.

SHE HAD FOLLOWED ME TO THE BATHROOM. I repeat, this little old lady had booked it down the church hallway in her Lavender Sunday suit complete with fascinator hat, to chase down a fleeing child. Somehow she found me hiding in the bathroom stall and sharply reprimanded me for running away from someone who "just wanted to give me a hug." Stunned, I stumbled out of hiding, reluctantly let her hug and pinch me, and hated every minute of it. I treaded slowly back to the sanctuary defeated and mad. I will never forget it. That old lady was NOT going to be denied her weekly church hug from the Pastor's daughter.

She wasn't a bad lady, she meant well, and I know she was lonely. But just because her motives weren't to harm me did not make it okay. I didn't need to yell at her, make her feel bad, or even make her agree with me. I just needed to be able to say "No thank you!"

I needed to be able to find a way to greet her and love her that was within my boundaries. I didn't have the skill set that I have now, but you can bet your sitter that I'll be teaching my future children that they can have their NO, and work to find ways to interact with people that they are comfortable with.

That stubborn fierce old lady has since gone on to heaven, and I know that when I get to see her in Glory, I will hug her, and truly be glad to see her. But I also know Jesus won't let her pinch my cheeks, because- boundaries, Sis!!!! Hallelujah.

IT'S TIME TO TAKE BACK YOUR NO

If there's one thing the South and the Bible Belt can produce like hotcakes, it is overworked, tired and run-down women. We've been taught our whole damn lives that we must always be sweet, and in order to always be sweet, one is never supposed to say NO.

NEVAAAAH, Dahlin. NEVAAAH.

"NO" is the most fundamental boundary a person can have, and if you don't have a "NO" then you don't have any boundaries. You have no sacred ground.

It does not matter what your reason is. There is never, ever a good enough reason to sacrifice your no. I realize that may sound pretty radical, and I know that even the thought of taking back your "no" makes some of you start dry heaving right away, but hear me out.

If we can't say "no," then we never really get to choose to say "yes," and if we don't ever get to choose, then our life is never really our own. When we don't own our lives, we are not showing up as all of who and how God made us to be, and we are walking in disobedience. In this place everything in our life *suffers*.

Everything. Our health, our marriages, our relationships, our finances, our careers, our mental health, and our children *suffer* when we won't say no.

Consider this: Boundaries come from God Himself. God does not force us to love Him, respect Him, or honor Him. One of the boundaries between us and God is that He is Holy and sin simply cannot stand in His presence. It's a spiritual law. We *all* have sin, so we cannot be in His presence. We are not perfect, but He is.

But because He loved us so much, He made a way through Jesus to take away our sin, so that we can be in His presence and live in close relationship with Him. He made a way for us to be washed clean and stand in His presence, *but we still have to choose Him*. We still have to choose the option He created for us. He does not force us.

Boundaries aren't fluff, high maintenance or unnecessary things just for people who have the luxury of more time to consider them. Boundaries are essential for your life on this earth. They are Godly and they define your sacred ground.

A life lived without boundaries, without a strong "no," is guaranteed to produce obligated, resentful, and uninspired women.... who eventually get so mad they burn things to the ground.

My journey back to finding myself and reclaiming my no was at times like the that scene from the finale of Game Of Thrones - a ticked off, crazed blonde girl on the back of an angry dragon burning an entire city to the ground.

But, oh Sis, the peace and joy that comes from finally finding and living in our boundaries, can open your life in a way you have never known before! You finally know what you're responsible for and what you're not. You are empowered to walk in full authority to stand your sacred ground, and you can freely release the things that are not yours to carry.

That'll preach.

"NO is a complete sentence."
- Anne Lamott

QUESTIONS

• Do you have a NO? Do you feel comfortable saying NO to people?

• Where is it hardest for you to say no?

• Where are you doing things you don't want to do?

• How can you begin to identify your sacred ground?

• Where do you thrive? Where do you feel good? What are you doing when you feel strong, empowered, and capable?

• Where do you crash? What are you doing when you feel stuck, like a victim, and without any personal boundaries?

• What can you choose to lay down today that's not your responsibility? (How others respond to your choices, other people's feelings, doing for others what they can and should be doing for themselves.)

CHAPTER 15
STAND YOUR SACRED GROUND

"Don't shrink, don't puff up, just stand your sacred ground."
-Brenè Brown

We *must* learn to stand in and protect our own sacred ground. The Yellowstone of our souls demands it.

When we live in our boundaries, we are at peace and able to be fully dedicated to what we alone are responsible for - ourselves. When we learn to stand our sacred ground, we are a *force*. We have a flow of resources, insight and energy that is nothing short of incredible. And we thrive, we don't just survive.

When we don't stand our sacred ground, we feel overrun and depleted. Frustration, anger, depression and exhaustion run our lives, and we are far from the radiant powerhouse we were created to be.

If you find yourself on the frustrated and resentful side today, chances are you have some boundary problems. The great news is, that's something you can fix.

Getting brutally clear on what is our responsibility and what is not, is some grown-ass woman work. Becoming fierce about owning the authority of our time, energy and bodies is our new calling. No longer enslaved to obligation, we can choose to give freely where we want to, and trust God with what we don't have to give. I can tell you from personal experience, that this can feel wildly radical and dangerous in a system that expects our total compliance. But damn if it doesn't also feel really, really good.

In a world where we can feel like a hurricane rages inside of us, while the *outside* world pushes, demands, and criticizes - we must learn to stand our sacred ground. We won't make it if we don't. Without boundaries, we're caught in the flood of whatever happens around us, while also drowning from the flood that can rise within us.

As High Strung Women, we have to find our healthy limits so we can establish boundaries both on the outside world and on our high-strung personalities. Healthy boundaries don't take away life or personal expression. They focus us and make us better by protecting us from ourselves and others.

HOLY GROUND

"Take Off Your Shoes, For You Are Standing On Holy Ground."
-God speaking to Moses in Exodus 3:5

Standing your sacred ground may sound extremely hokey to you. It may sound like something that a girl named Skye who wears a dress made of hemp and hasn't showered in months would say to you while offering you a magic brownie. But, hear me out.

When something is considered "sacred," it is held with great respect, it is considered holy and it is believed to have a special connection with God.

I'm about to get real excited, so buckle up. Sis, when we live within our boundaries and stand our sacred ground, we throw open the door to a much more powerful connection to the God of the Universe!!!! I love this principle so much because it's not complicated or mystic.

We will always find greater peace, clarity in hearing God, and know more power when we stand our sacred ground and honor our boundaries. It's an act of obedience.

Life is just so much better standing on your sacred ground.

Living with boundaries reduces the noise in our lives. It focuses us, settles us and frees us. It protects us from being distracted by things that are not ours to carry, focuses us on what is really important and helps us use our energy and resources for the right things. It puts us in a space to make the best decisions and do our best work, free from the snare of how others might react. That's their business, but this right here- This.Is.Mine.

Let's stop and be honest for a second, Do you consider any part of your life, your body or yourself with holy respect, regard or protection? To consider it sacred?

I know I didn't. Holiness was something I believed happened *outside of me.* It was reserved for church or spiritual matters. Frankly, for things that were kind of intimidating and scary, and ultimately things that I didn't understand.

We have seen what happens when we don't regard any part of ourselves as sacred. We don't have to look far to see the effects of a life lived in last place on the priority list. Sis, you and I were made for far more than last place. It's time to step up, to show up for ourselves.

No one is more important than you. No one is more deserving of care, rest or boundaries than you. Some may say this is outrageously narcissistic, but it is *not.* This is a deeply humble place where we acknowledge our assignment from God (ourselves), and we abandon trying to be God in anyone's life. Oh Sis, there is so much rest when we quit trying to be God.

ADDICTED TO APPROVAL

I'm not sure that there's a bright side to people pleasing, but there is absolutely a dark side. When we live our lives more concerned with other people than ourselves- trying to please them, control them, or protect them, the only non-negotiable we have in our lives is trying harder to make them happy. We become a slave to it - working when we don't want to and giving when we don't have anything left to give. We become filled to the brim with resentment. We are compelled by our unfulfilled needs of acceptance, affirmation and approval to do whatever it takes to make them "happy" with us. Rooted in this belief system is the fantasy that if "they" are happy with me, then I will finally be happy with me.

I call it a fantasy because it IS. It's just as much of a fairytale as a leprechaun riding a unicorn holding a laser-cat running on a rainbow road through clouds of cotton candy in space. If you're working and waiting for someone to tell you that you're good enough, and believing that it will slay all your inner demons, you're gonna die waiting Sis.

The problem with living for other people's approval is that at any given moment, no matter what we are doing or how well we are doing it, we are being filtered through someone else's mental, physical, emotional and spiritual state -

and most people are crazy as hell.

Live accordingly.

When we are living for other people's approval nothing is sacred. We sacrifice ourselves at the altar of someone else's opinion, and we find ourselves at the mercy of whatever mood, whim or psychological problem others push on us. But true FREEDOM comes when we realize that other people's opinions are neither our responsibility nor our business.

We can weather conflict much easier when we realize that most of how people act toward us isn't about us at all, it's about them. We should always be mindful of our words, actions and choices, but we should never be a slave to winning people over.

We will never win everyone over. It is impossible. We are responsible for us. God is responsible for everyone else. We'll be worn out and mad when we try to control the worlds' response to us. People are gonna be in whatever mood they are going to be in no matter what you do, so let them be in it and walk on. Don't forget, when you stand your sacred ground and focus on your responsibility, you are in the powerful place of obedience. You are protected by God, and He will handle your reputation and everyone else. He's got you Sis, and He can handle the haters.

Defining and enforcing the boundaries in your life *will* have a sorting effect on the people in your life. Some will get it and some won't. The second batch will get mad because they don't understand, and they'll probably call you selfish. But you know what? They don't have to understand or agree with you for it to be right for you.

It can be rough to let people go, but sometimes it is absolutely necessary. Releasing those who don't understand or won't honor your boundaries can be rough, but it is critical for your personal growth. Letting those people go enables us to connect with others from a new place of choice, health and maturity and the result is life changing.

I don't just like people now, I LOVE MY PEOPLE. I trust them to love me and respect my boundaries, and they trust me to do the same. Our interactions are not filled with nervousness, hidden feelings or anxiety. Instead we belly laugh, share brave truths and love each other right where we are. Even when we don't agree.

THE FREEDOM TO CHOOSE

Up until Ryan, I had approached most of my previous relationships from a place of insecurity and fear. I lived out of a "will *you be the one* who *finally* loves me?" mindset. I trust you are familiar with the inevitable woes that follow from this kind of panicked dating. But I eventually discovered the profound mental shift to "I wonder if he will be the one who *gets* to love me and be loved by me?" and I was forever changed.

If that sounds prideful to you, I'm afraid you're missing it. One comes from a place of desperation, a victim that needs to be rescued from feeling unloved. The second comes from a place of value, confidence, and partnership.

After Ryan and I had been dating a while, my Dad asked how things were going with the two of us. At one point in the conversation, my father, ever the romantic, said, "Well, Ab, can you live without him?"

Surprised, I looked back at him and slowly said, "Well yes. I can live without him... but I don't know that I *want* to."

That may not sound very romantic to you, but you need to know something from this extremely codependent, highly addicted-to-people-pleasing, insecure woman. THIS was the first time I had shifted from a panicked place of looking for affirmation, to knowing my own worth and leading my own life. I was now able to choose, CHOOSE where I wanted to be, with whom I wanted to be and *how* I wanted to be with someone.

What we willingly *choose* is always stronger than what we force ourselves to go along with out of fear of what we'll lose if we don't. I've done it both ways, and having the freedom and room to choose changes everything. It released a kind of love I had never known.

Ryan didn't crush or reprimand my strong spirit. He ran alongside me grinning and made me run faster. He is truly a king among men - brilliant, handsome, brave and strong, and he calls me higher and farther just by being himself.

Even though I was terrified at times of how much I loved and was drawn to him, I *wanted* to choose him. I didn't marry him because I needed someone to take care of me financially or because I was afraid of being alone. I married him because I wanted to, and even though I could survive without him, I didn't *want* to live without him.

So on July 4, 2008, in a small, French stone chapel on the Riverwalk in San Antonio, Texas in front of our friends and

146

family: I chose Peter Ryan Petkoff forever, and he chose me. On the hard days and on the best days, we can look each other in the eye and know that we are here because we chose to be, we want to be.

In my opinion this is one of the ways that Christ loving the church is fleshed out in marriage. Jesus didn't need us. God didn't have to have us. We were unholy, sinful, stuck in bondage and far from what He created us to be.

But you know what? He wanted us. He CHOSE us, and when we choose Him- we are forever changed.

THE GOLDEN RULE IN BOUNDARIES

A powerful starting point when it comes to learning about our boundaries is what I like to call the "Golden Rule of Boundaries." It's actually based on one of my least favorite Bible verses (let's be honest- we all have at least one), *"Give with a cheerful heart,"* out of 2 Corinthians 9:7.

In their book "Boundaries In Marriage," Cloud and Townsend teach on "Give with a cheerful heart," in a way that forever changed my life.

Instead of the heavy, dutiful message of: you better be willing to give all that you have, and you better be happy ("cheerful") about it! Cloud and Townsend teach this revolutionary and simple principle, based on the *full* scripture of 2 Corinthians 9:7.

If you cannot give with a cheerful heart, then....
DO NOT GIVE.

When we give when we don't want to, it becomes a gift with strings attached to it, and that is not truly a gift.

HERE'S THE KICKER: when we give when we don't want to, and then resent it later.... it's OUR OWN FAULT!

THIS is a big part of finding, and standing our sacred

ground. When you cannot give something - whether you have been asked or you just feel the expectation to give, but you cannot give it freely, with no expectations for a return-DON'T DO IT. Don't you dare. This is how we stand our sacred ground and trust God with the rest.

I think you'll find the full context of 2 Corinthians 9:7 below rather interesting. I know I did.

"Each of you should give what you have decided in your heart to give. You shouldn't give if you don't want to. You shouldn't give because you are forced to. God loves a cheerful giver."
2 Corinthians 9:7 NIRV

"She set her boundaries and rebuilt her life."
-Cara Alwill Leyba

QUESTIONS

• Do you give when you don't want to?

• What are some of those places, circumstances?

• How can you practice saying NO when you need to?

• How can you embrace and celebrate saying YES when you want to?

• What would you like to say YES more to?

• What pushes you past your healthy limits? How can you stop allowing this to happen?

• What are the limits you find you work best within? (Example: 8 hours of sleep a night, a firm cutoff time for your workday, 48 hour visits back home to see family, 1 hour lunches with a friend who complains too much etc.)

CHAPTER 16
NATURAL CONSEQUENCES

"Some people create their own storms then get mad when it rains."

-Unknown

I once had a friend who nannied for a family in town with a 3-year-old little boy and a brand new baby girl. The little boy had recently hit a new phase of acting out: in protest to missing his mom, dealing with a new little sister and discovering the strong will of a growing toddler. He was more than trying my sweet friend's patience, not to mention her nannying skills, but this kid shocked us all with his next move.

One morning, while out with his nanny and little sister at a park, he decided that even though he was well past potty training, he would pull his pants down and poop under a tree.

Yes, you read that right - this little guy popped a squat, bared his naked booty, and pooped under a tree in the middle of a very crowded public park in a nice part of Dallas. Even as I was hearing my friend tell this story I could not stop laughing.

Shocked, completely grossed out but still trying not to give him any indication of her bewilderment, she asked herself, "Okay, what are the natural consequences of this action? What are the natural consequences of … pooping under a tree in a public place?"

The boy's parents had encouraged her to use natural consequences as a means of discipline, so after great debate, she decided the best option was to find a bag, and walk him over so he could pick up his own poop and throw it away. He strongly objected, of course, but SuperNanny stood strong. After facing the consequences of his actions, they went straight to the bathroom, washed everyone's hands three times and had a strong discussion about the importance of using toilets at all times.

That discussion must have made extra sense to the little boy that day, who learned that, when you don't poop in the toilet, you have to pick it up yourself.

Why on earth am I sharing a funny and gross story about a raging 3-year-old going rogue with his bathroom business? Because this was the first time the idea of "natural consequences" was introduced to me, and I.Was.Fascinated.

Up to that point in my life, I had felt held responsible for the actions and feelings of others. It had always been my job to try and alleviate, and it seemed downright heretical not to intervene or try and fix. But natural consequences also sounded beautifully radical to me: kind of like hope and a lot like freedom.

Natural consequences are what naturally happen as a result of something that we do. The inevitable consequence to an action. For example, if you punch the wall because you're mad, you hurt your hand. The natural consequence of pain serves as motivation not to punch the wall the next time you are angry. For our purposes here, think of it like cause and effect in relationships.

Some examples include:
- When we're mean to people, they don't want to be around us anymore.
- When we abuse people or things, we lose access to them.
- When we spend all our money on shoes, we can't pay our bills.

Natural consequences are how we learn to live within our

boundaries, and how we learn to respect the boundaries of others. But problems arise when we start to intervene, smooth over, or alleviate natural consequences for others.

When I was in high school, one of my best friends was a lifeguard at her neighborhood pool during the summer. We'll call her "Kristy," because thanks to the *Baby Sitters Club* books, I always wanted a friend named Kristy.

At the same time I had a summer job as a kids camp counselor at a sports camp at our church, and we were both thrilled to finally be making our own money to go to the movies, cruise Gadzooks at the mall, or hit up TCBY on summer nights.

But three months into the school year, she had spent all of her summer earnings. So when it came time to go do something fun, she would always say, "Ugh I can't go. I don't have any money and my mom won't give me any."

Desperate for some fun, and always ready to take on any extra responsibility, I would offer to pay her way into the movies, for dinner, or whatever else we were trying to get into that day. She'd gladly take me up on the offer, and off we'd go, living our best life in the late 90s, rocking our jorts, puka-shell necklaces and bad

Sun-In highlights.

My dad eventually wised up to what was going on, and sat me down for a little convo.

He asked why I was always paying Kristy's way when we went out. He knew she'd had a summer job too. In fact, her job paid better than mine. I told him she had spent all her money from being a lifeguard, and she couldn't go out if I didn't help her.

He gently said he understood why I wanted to have a friend to go do fun things with, but then he dropped a truth bomb on my freshman self, as only my father-the-pastor could: "Ab, you may be getting in God's way."

Instantly nervous, and a little nauseous, I whispered that I didn't understand.

He said that perhaps God was trying to work with Kristy on how to manage her money and to teach her some things. But every time I paid for her, I was getting in the way of what He might be trying to show her. Kristy didn't have a problem because I kept solving it for her.

Oy. Vey.

By constantly paying her way, I was removing the natural consequences of her choices and hindering an important life lesson. If you spend all your money, you don't have any left to go do fun things later on. You feel sad, left out, and disappointed. Feeling that way helps teach us and motivate us to manage our money.

Now, 15-year-old me was not about to get in God's way, so I shut that down fast. She was kind of mad, I was disappointed and we definitely missed out on some bad rom-coms and mall cruising as a result. But I much preferred knowing I wasn't interfering with the Almighty.

This radical truth also applies to our boundaries.

When we remove the natural consequences for people who have crossed our boundaries, we work against the very tools God uses to teach and grow them.

When we act like it's fine that our spacey friend flaked again on our coffee date, when we make excuses for our spouse who isn't pulling his weight around the house, or when we put up with someone talking down to us because they're "just like that," Sis, consider this: you are getting in God's way.

The natural consequences of not showing up to a coffee date, especially repeatedly? You realize that friend doesn't value your time as much as hers, so you don't reschedule. You let that girl go in love, and refocus your time on someone who respects your time and honors her commitments. She and God will work it out, and chances are, she'll learn to value people's time if she wants to have friends. You aren't there to teach her a lesson, you're just there to honor your boundaries - God teaches the lessons. Don't get that twisted.

The natural consequence for not pulling your weight

around the house as a spouse can be living in a mess and the toll frustration takes on the relationship. Don't avoid that conflict. Trust me, you're going to be mad regardless. Talk it out. If you keep making it okay for him - by doing all his chores for him, he doesn't even know it's a problem. He doesn't HAVE to know. I'm gonna go ahead and say it: let him have no clean underwear. If he can't put them in the hamper, then he can wear dirties. When you keep making it okay, it becomes your problem instead of his.

The natural consequence for someone talking down to us should be immediate rebuttal, walking away, or severely limiting or ending your interaction/exposure to them completely. By standing up to them and walking away - you communicate you will not tolerate their behavior, and they need to learn how to speak to you differently if they want to have any type of conversation with you.

God uses natural consequences as a wake up call. This is true both ways, Sis. When we demand others fix our problems, pay our way or minimize the damage, we are asking them to take responsibility for what is not theirs. We are asking them to stand in God's way.

I'm proud to say my girl Kristy is now a badass budgeting genius mom who not only lives within her means, but has also started a thriving side business to earn extra income. Part of her testimony is how God has provided for her and her family financially. Look at all God can do when we trust Him and get out of the way!

The foundation of a natural consequence is that a person experiences the weight of their own actions and realizes they alone can fix it. They alone are responsible. Contrary to our fears, this is not mean or cruel.

Handing people's problems back to them empowers them, and frees you up from their mess.

That's the kind of truth and real life application that will get this girl out of her church pew and dancing in the aisle with her tambourine!!!!!! (Just kidding- I don't have a tambourine, but guuuurrrrl if I did!!!)

OBEDIENCE

Boundaries are an act of *obedience* to God, and there are a boatload of blessings when we walk in obedience. I get all hyped up (in a good way) about obedience because it is often a highly misunderstood and misinterpreted idea. Growing up, especially at church, I always heard about obedience as "you better obey, *or else...*" Motivation by fear is certainly effective for a time, but it is hardly the heart of God. **God does not threaten, He reigns.**

What we choose to do willingly is always more powerful than what we cower to do out of fear. Faith and fear resonate in completely different energies in the spirit realm.

I'm gonna say that again, Sis: what we choose to do out of faith and what we submit to in fear resonate on opposite ends of the spectrum in the spirit realm. One is power (faith), and one is force (fear).

Believe it or not, one of the best ways I ever heard obedience taught was actually by a guest speaker in youth group. She described obeying God and the authorities God has placed over us, like standing under the protection of a big umbrella. Under the umbrella we are safe, protected, and able to rest. We're at peace with God. But when we disobey God, or our parents (as teenagers), we step out from under the protection of the umbrella and into the storm.

She then gave everyone's favorite youth-group-sermon-teaching-example: sneaking out of your house to go to a party that you had been forbidden to go to. Here's what she said: when you sneak out of that house, get into a car with your friends and head to that party- you have stepped out of God's protection and your parents protection as well. You are now at the mercy of a teenage driver on a highway who could wreck at any moment, a high school house party with alcohol that could be raided by the police, and because you snuck out, no one even knows you're gone to come looking for you if you get hurt or in trouble.

THAT made a lot more sense to me and was far more motivating to me as a teenager than "you better obey, or else!" Obedience protects us, puts the pressure back on God, and allows us to walk in peace, finding rest from anxiety.

Honoring our boundaries isn't just fluff, it is obedience to care for what He has given us and trust Him with the rest. But when we aren't living in our boundaries, when we are running around all up in everyone's else's business, we are walking in *disobedience*. We've stepped out from under that umbrella of God's protection, and things start flying at us. This truth should cause us to become even more fierce about holding onto our boundaries, because is there ever a good enough reason to disobey God? I think you know the answer to that.

This isn't about legalism and never messing up. We will never get it right every time. We'll get off track and have to find our way back, and God knows that about us. He always welcomes us home with open arms. This is about challenging the lie that we should have no boundaries, and for many of us - it's going to take a strong push to make that change.

If God considers holding my boundaries to be obedience, then I become a lot more confident saying no or letting people experience the natural consequences of their actions.

When you've lost your way, and have gotten wrapped up in pleasing others- girl, you run like hell back to your sacred ground, the holy ground of obedience. Obedience in your boundaries.

He will meet you there, and you will find peace once again in your sacred ground. You know what is yours to carry and you know what is His. You take time to review what God says you are responsible for (YOU), and what you're not (literally everything else). You lay down the extra weight, trust Him with the outcome, and carry on only worrying about yo-self and nobody else.

No longer panicked and fearful, we can walk clearly and confidently into our futures.

QUESTIONS

• How can you begin to honor and respect your own sacred ground?

• Where have you been doing things out of guilt and not choice?

• Where are you blocking natural consequences for others?

• How can you begin to allow others to experience the weight of their own choices, moods, or words?

CHAPTER 17
BUT WHAT DO I DO WHEN...

Let's Talk Real-Life Boundaries

After the last few chapters, you may be thinking, "Alright, Ab. All that boundary stuff sounds great, but Lord have mercy, WHAT DO I SAY? WHAT DO I DO? I need talking points, an outline, something! I'm already nervous and nauseous just thinking about how the hell to tell people no! Help!"

Sis, I got you.

Let's talk some real-life examples that we deal with on the regular as women. For the next few pages, consider me your personal hype girl, helping you feel confident, brave, and able to walk with swagger to own your boundaries! I'm gonna talk you UP sis. You can do this. You are a badass and your world needs you to have your boundaries so you can show up in all of your glory! We are about to do the damn thing.

Let's say you find yourself in the following situations:

"Man, I just don't have it to listen to Lindsey vent about her boss again today..." Or, "I don't know that I can afford to be a bridesmaid for Amanda. I am fighting to get a hold of my finances and pay off my debt."

We're gonna start here: SIS, LISTEN TO YOUR GUT. Not your guilt. Not your fears. Listen to that primal, holy instinct that lives in your bones.

No matter what you hear when you listen in, refuse to judge

or shame yourself. As women we have been programmed to doubt ourselves and fear our strong reactions, always assuming that we need to be tempered. But that is precisely how we get so far off track. We must stop judging and start listening. We need to give our feelings a seat at our table, and let them tell us their story.

I have long been fascinated by this truth: the root of suffering is resistance. We suffer tremendously when we refuse and resist our true instinct and feelings. Instead of shaming ourselves into doing things we don't really want to do, we will save ourselves so much trouble and mess if we simply listen to and honor our true feelings.

"Suck it up and just be nice" dishonors both you and those you are pretending for. When we deny our gut, and go against our true feelings- it just never goes well. The truth has a way of always coming out.

Here are some ways we can begin to listen to our instincts and honor our boundaries.

REAL LIFE EXAMPLE #1
Friend That Complains To You NonStop.
"Man, I really don't have it to listen to Lindsey vent about her boss again today…"

We all have at least one person in our lives that loves to talk more than do. We also all have a limited amount of grace and room to listen to someone complain, not because we are bad people, but because we ALL have limits. Please hear me on this - listening to someone complain should *never* be an inexhaustible resource. That is unrealistic, and ultimately it does not help the one complaining.

When you find you've reached your limit of sympathy-marathon-listening, your gut is saying ENOUGH. Honor it. Listen as long as you can give your time freely and happily. But when you hit your limit, listen up. That's your boundary talking.

Perhaps you are caught in a relationship pattern where you are enabling Lindsey to vent, and not DO. Venting can be helpful in some places, but it is not a long-term strategy to getting happy.

Venting over an extended period of time does not empower the person for action to actually change what they are frustrated with. Venting without action only grows their *frustration.*

VENTING IS NOT A LONG TERM STRATEGY TO GETTING HAPPY.

Let's be honest: venting is just a word we use to make "complaining" sound better. We all need to vent from time to time, but if venting has become a practice, a habit when things get rough, it's time to make a change.

Alight, so here is one way to approach this situation: Lindsey calls, and you listen. Lindsey calls again, and again, and you listen, listen. But then, at some point you realize you have reached your "limit" with rehashing the same issues every day on your drive home from work. You hate that your friend is in a tough place, and you want to be supportive, but it's casting a negative, victim-mindset, can't-get-out mentality over your life and leaves you feeling heavy. Real talk here: **you don't like it.** (Listen to your gut girl- do it!!!)

So the next time Lindsey calls and starts in on how bad her boss was today, you can say something like this:

"Linds, I am so sorry you are so frustrated. I really hate that you feel so unappreciated and manipulated by your boss. I know how good you are at your job and what an amazing woman you are. I want to be an encouragement to you, but I'm afraid I really can't help you here. You need to be able to talk to someone who can really help you make progress

towards a solution! I so want you to find your happy again! I love you, and I support you! On that note, would you be free to meet up with some other girls this weekend for a happy hour? I think it'd be really good to get out and laugh!"

You kindly communicated that you hear and validate her frustrations - how you love and value her - but also that you have reached your limit with being able to help. You encouraged her toward actionable steps, while also set a firm boundary on your time.

If she takes steps towards action and change, then awesome! If she doesn't, then you honor your boundary, reminding her that you can't help her here and redirect the conversation. Eventually, you may have to limit your exposure to her if she keeps complaining. This may look like not answering your phone every time she calls. I know that can sound incredibly scary, but honor your limit, stand your sacred ground here, and trust God with both your friendship and with His work in Lindsey.

Although this may sound harsh to some, it is extremely rational and true. When we find that someone we love chronically complains and refuses to act on what is in their power alone to fix, then why should we invest our time to continue to listen? The truth is at this point they are choosing to suffer, but you don't have to choose to suffer with them.

You can love them and let them be where they are, but you cannot fix them, or fix it for them. Healthy boundaries demand that we hand problems that are not our own back to their rightful owner.

After 43 years of marriage, when my Dad is in a bad way, my Mom has learned to say to him: "I know you are frustrated and angry. I am so sorry you feel that way, and I hurt for you. You can be down in that pit as long as you want to, but I am not crawling down in there with you."

I may not have been raised by the softest woman, but damn if she doesn't speak some truth!

You got this Sis- listen to your gut, honor your limits, stand your sacred ground!

REAL LIFE EXAMPLE #2
Trying To Figure Out What You Can
& Can't Give Freely

"I don't know that I can afford to be a bridesmaid for Amanda right now. I am fighting to get a hold of my finances and pay off my debt."

(Also applicable for baby showers, birthday extravaganzas, girls trips, etc.)

Healthy boundaries help us define what we can and cannot freely give.

Sis, you are the only one who knows what would push you past your limits personally, financially and relationally. You can't make anyone else responsible for that, so we have to tune in and get honest. We must reject the lie that really loving someone means we can never tell them "no." That's not love, that's fear.

FILTERING TO FIND YOUR HAPPY-GIVER-HEART WHEN FACING A DECISION

1. Start with what you actually WANT to do, not what other people want you to do or need you to do. What do you truly want to do?
2. From the list of things that you actually want to do, begin to filter out what you know you CAN'T do that would break or push your boundaries financially, emotionally, or physically.
3. You will then start to see what you CAN do- what you can give freely and with a happy heart!

Some of us will want to do everything, so this filtering process is important. What you will find at the end of this process is what you can give freely. You want to give it, and you can do so without dishonoring your own boundaries.

Now, back to our real-life example of being asked to be a bridesmaid. Of course you love your friend, Amanda, the bride-to-be, and you want to celebrate with her! But we must put in the work to find what we can and cannot do, so we can love her and give freely and not be resentful later.

Even though you may want to do everything fun she's asked you to be a part of, you find your truth as you lean into the details: you cannot honor your financial boundaries and afford to do everything on her list.

Sure- you could stretch yourself, max out a credit card, and make other areas of your life suffer in order to "make" it happen for Amanda, but that's not standing your sacred ground. Loving Amanda well does not require loving yourself less. And remember, when we don't stand our sacred ground - we are walking in disobedience, and we suffer. Our friendship will suffer in the long run as well, resentment is a sticky bitch. She's really tough to get rid of once she takes hold in our hearts.

SO HERE'S HOW YOU WORK IT OUT

You must clearly define what you want to do, and can do. "I want to, and can save for and afford to buy the bridesmaid dress Amanda has chosen, and I can take the time off of work for the wedding weekend. But I cannot afford to fly to Vegas and take three more days off work for her bachelorette party. I don't want to be in the hole after this wedding!" Once you have defined specifically what you can and can't do, talk to Jesus about it, and trust Him to have your back as you talk to Amanda.

Here is a nugget of truth I have learned the hard way: when discussing what you can and can't do, do NOT go in with general, wide sweeping statements. Things like "it's just too much," "I can't do it all," or "you're asking too much of me." Those comments are like Dolly Parton walking by an open flame in one of her best wigs covered in AquaNet. Things will escalate fast.

Don't do it.

Instead, get specific about what you can and can't do (actual events, financial commitments, dates), and take those very specific things to your conversation. Start with what you are EXCITED about and happy to get to celebrate with her! Focus on the fact that you love her, you are honored to be a part of her wedding, and then clearly communicate what she can count on you for.

Let me stop and acknowledge that getting specific and setting a healthy boundary like this requires a tremendous amount of courage - especially to those of us who loathe confrontation. But it is a challenge that will serve you well in the long run. Leave no room for confusion, be upfront but kind and you will experience far less drama in your life - guaranteed.

Ask to meet with Amanda discreetly and privately. Bonus tip: Don't text her with vague and moody vibes. Be upbeat, positive, and refuse to get into anything until you can meet in person. When you do get together, begin with how much you love her and how excited you are to celebrate with her! THEN with THE SAME amount of conviction and authority- communicate clearly to her what you can do, and what you cannot do. If you want to, you can share your priority of managing your finances and how important that is to you - but it's up to you.

Now, even though you may feel like you should, you don't have to grovel or be sorry. It's important for your posture to be confident and loving. You don't have to tell her all of why, she doesn't need to know every detail, and she most certainly doesn't have to agree with your decision in order for it to be the right thing for you to do.

Your job here is to clearly communicate what she can count on you for with great joy, and where you're unavailable with great conviction.

Don't you dare lie or make up some flimsy excuse. You are better than that, and your friend deserves better than that. Don't tell her you can do it all out of fear and then just not show up or bail at the last minute. That's not an accident, that's intentional and really crappy.

Don't be a coward here Sis- those are the worst kind of friends. You can do this! You are learning how to be an excellent friend- both to yourself and those you love. It may feel intimidating, but it is nothing less than badass!!!

Your sacred ground looks like refusing to to compromise your boundaries out of fear, and finding the joy of giving what you can happily give. This is an exceptional gift- for it honors you as the giver and the one you love. That is a much deeper gift than surface compliance. Not everyone will see it as such, but God does and He will bless it.

The same application could be made if relationally, you love Lauren the bride, but her bridesmaid tribe and general wedding approach just wear you out. It is "more than you can afford" or want to give, in *another way* (that's a whole other sermon that could preach itself). Maybe it's way too much of the "Woo-Girl" parties, they can drink Irishmen under the table, or the bridesmaid vibe is super Mean Girls and it stresses you out.

Sis, you do not have to do *all* of the things- every shower, every event, every single moment to prove that you love someone and are a good friend. Give what you can give FREELY and happily (no place for guilt or BS here). Let the rest go.

Now, if she is in a good space herself, she will likely do her best to understand and support you, even if she is disappointed. If she totally doesn't get it and blows up, well

Sis, this may be one of those defining moments in your friendship. I know weddings have made and broken many relationships in my own life. I don't know what it is about them, but Lawwwwd, if weddings don't make people CRAZY! Or perhaps, weddings just reveal the truth. As my girl Allison says, "I can't know," but they are like a cutting knife.

The big win here is that even if she's crazy or mad, you are OKAY. Better yet sis- you're thriving, because you have stood your sacred ground, which means you have been OBEDIENT to your Father!

Amanda may not get it, she may get mad. But you can trust God with your reputation, and you are still working at what He's called you to do. Your life, your sanity and your resources haven't been derailed by the fear of what one person will think of you!

You stood your sacred ground.

Hallelujah.

*Now, if she **does get it**-* I can't even begin to tell you the joy that swells from your heart to get to love and celebrate a friend in the way that you can and want to, that is within what you have chosen to give freely, and happily. When you do it that way, it's like your happy just explodes and expands - because you are giving the right way, and God is blessing it, multiplying it. Yes He does that! Giving with a truly happy heart to give, only breeds more happy!!!

CARING WORKS- CARETAKING DOESN'T
- Melody Beattie

Having boundaries and choosing ourselves does not mean we are supposed to become heartless, selfish, narcissistic people. We are to care for those around us - to love them, without trying to fix them.

We must learn to let others be right where they are, and how they are. Life is messy, and it can be hard to watch those we love struggle through things, but we must refuse to step in God's way. *You have so much more to give to this world than rescuing others from their messes.* They are going to be alright, and it's time to aim higher than just being on call for other peoples self-imposed disasters.

Walking out real life boundaries comes down to these key places:
- Knowing and defining our limits, our boundaries.
- Giving only what we can give freely.
- Allowing others to be where they are.
- Allowing the natural consequences of choices to flow unhindered.
- Trusting God to do His work in all of our lives.

We are no longer panicked, afraid or tortured. We are steady, measured and boldly confident that God will have His way in our lives.

That'll preach Sis.

PART IV

Emotions

CHAPTER 18
EMOTIONAL WOMAN, DANGEROUS WOMAN.

"The woman who allows her emotions to flow freely is dangerous, but not because she is going to lose it. She is dangerous because she has been LOOSED from the shackles of fearful control and freed up to walk forth in all of her power and insight. No longer afraid of herself, she harnesses the strength of her big emotions to do big things."

In an instant, I can feel my face flush. The surge of adrenaline and feeling rush through my body, and the electricity of what is awakening inside of me flashes in my muscles. I take a deep breath and hold on.

Here come my emotions.

They scare me. They excite me. They clear my mind.

After being held back for so long, my feelings rush in fast and strong. I feel nervous, but relieved, because as I allow my feelings, I find clarity. Things that seemed hidden from me are now revealed. My feelings rattle my bones and wake my soul every time I let them flow. They bring me back to life, and back to myself, and I am grateful.

I haven't always felt this way about my emotions, and I still struggle daily. But I have come to learn that the emotional torment we can experience as women isn't because our feelings are bad, it's because we haven't known what the hell to do with them. We don't fully understand them, and so we awkwardly swing back and forth between emotional extremes

171

until we finally just shut them all down.

A woman ruled by her emotions is chaotic and volatile, but a woman cut off from her emotions becomes cold and rigid. So how are we to live?

Somewhere along the way, someone decided (let's be honest, probably a man) that having and showing our feelings made us weak, made us unstable, made us … human. I think it's safe to say that whoever outlawed emotions was probably someone who decided they made him too uncomfortable.

Like many of you, I spent most of my life in a panicked grip trying to push them down, absolutely terrified of what they might make me do. I spent most of my energy every day trying to manage the hurricane raging inside of my chest, and it was *exhausting*.

As High Strung Women, we have ALL of the feelings, all of the time. I swear we experience more emotions on a daily basis than some men do in a decade. We don't have little feelings. We have *BIG* feelings, and we have them all the time.

I don't know about you, but I have *never* been able to hide how I feel to save my life. Even if I set my mind to it, my face simply refuses to cooperate. I *always* feel strongly. Even when I'm not sure what I'm feeling, I feel very strongly about not being sure about what I am feeling. (My husband is somewhere right now shouting a loud "AMEN" to that statement! Hah!)

My world taught me early on that my emotions, the very things that make me distinctly human and profoundly female, were nothing but trouble. I was taught that to cry, especially in public, meant that I should be ashamed. I was taught that to grieve, to be inconsolable, was embarrassing. I was taught that to be excited was not cool. I was taught that to be broken-hearted wasn't attractive, and that to be filled with passion and determination was intimidating and off-putting to others.

But I was taught to fear and distrust my big emotions the most. My big emotions were treated like the dangerous and forbidden "Pandora's Box." They had me convinced that anyone who dared to open my big emotions would be met with a sobbing, shrieking monster who would embarrass us all to no end.

No wonder we are so deeply disconnected from both ourselves and our incredible emotional intuition as women.

Today we see lost, uninspired women who careen back and forth - stumbling in a numb shuffle, to drowning in rage. Feeling nothing has become safer to us than feeling anything at all. But by shutting down our emotions, we are starving our high strung personalities and dying a slow, sad death.

I can see it, can you? This is undeniably the handiwork of our enemy. His fingerprints are all over oppression and self rejection. He works day and night to keep us in conflict with ourselves. He's no fool. He knows that a healthy woman connected to her emotions can become a spiritual force that will rattle the heavens. But he is not going to win.

This will come as no surprise by now, but as our emotions are a force unlike any other, our answer lies in the messy, beautiful pursuit of mastery. We are going to learn how to partner with our emotions and start to experience them as the superpower that they were created to be.

Today we begin the spiritual work of reconciling with our emotions, understanding their role and limits, and learning to honor their profound place in our lives as High Strung Women. Today, we take back one of the greatest gifts God gave us- our superpower.

GOD CREATED US IN HIS IMAGE TO FEEL

Our emotions aren't some troubling byproduct of being human. They were intentionally designed by God to connect us to Him, to ourselves, and to the world around us in a very powerful way.

We are made in His image, and because He feels, so do we.

Scripture reveals over and over God's own emotions. He weeps. He gets angry. He delights in joy.

To feel our emotions is to be alive, and to share our emotions with God and others connects us to them in a way nothing else can. How much stronger is your connection to someone when you can hear the pain in their voice or see the joy in their eyes? You could receive the same information on a piece of paper with no emotion attached to it and experience little to no connection to it's author. Emotions *connect* us.

There is no greater testament to the importance of emotions in the life of a healthy human than spending an hour with a child. I have four nephews under the age of 6, and their boundless joy, unbridled sorrow and electric excitement are so pure that they have made me weep. To watch them live so fully moment by moment, took the breath of my soul away. I didn't realize until I saw it, how much I was pushing my own emotions down, and how it had numbed me to this one life I have been given.

We're surrounded by a world doing it's best not to feel anything. But *what if* we couldn't feel anything? What if we couldn't fall in love? What if our hearts could not swell with joy the first time we heard "Mama?" What if we couldn't sob, and shake, and grieve at the loss of someone we felt so much for? Someone we loved so deeply we can't bear to breathe without?

Although our feelings can scare and intimidate us, they are one of the best parts of our humanity. Don't be afraid of the work here Sis, it's messy, but good. `

QUESTIONS:

- What were you taught about being emotional growing up?

- What were you taught about you own emotions as a woman in your family?

- Do you overvalue or undervalue your feelings?

- How can you begin to allow your feelings to tell you their story?

- How can you start to see your emotions as your superpower?

CHAPTER 19
HIGH DEFINITION INTUITION

"Her intuition was her favorite superpower."

-Unknown

GASOLINE AND MATCHES

If our passionate personalities are the powerful engine that drive us as High Strung Women, then our emotions and our feelings are the fuel. Our emotions are a tremendous source of energy and insight, and our feelings affect more of what we do than most of us realize. The powerful combination of our spirited personalities and big emotions are what make us so special as High Strung Women.

They are gasoline and matches. They are the right combination of forces to power an incredible machine or they can blow the whole place up! As High Strung Women, working with high octane forces is just part of our life. We know we must learn to harness these forces for our good.

For our purposes here, I will use emotions and feelings interchangeably. A deeper dive into psychology would show a marked difference between the two, but since we are focused on addressing overall emotional health and wellness, I feel this distinction would only be distracting. I am not a therapist, a doctor or a mental-health professional. I am just a High Strung Woman who has struggled deeply with my emotions, and have searched the world over for help and insight. I have thrown myself into books, listening to experts and my own therapy to try to understand these forces that surge in my chest - and I am here to simply share things that have helped me.

Our emotions are an undeniable force that we have misunderstood and pushed away for far too long. But just because we have denied them, does not mean they have been denied.

We can ignore a feeling, but that does not erase it. That emotion continues to operate on a subconscious level, and affects us deeply. That's part of why they are so powerful. Even when we try to bury our emotions, they are still at work inside of us. So rather than war against them the rest of our lives, we must learn to befriend them and work with them. The amazing thing is- your emotions are *for you* in a way that no one else ever could be. They serve you and you alone, and what they have to offer you in friendship is stunning. They can be complex and deeply misunderstood, much like you and I, but they are more than worth the work.

OUR EMOTIONS ARE MESSENGERS

Our emotions serve as messengers from our subconscious. They tell us how we *really feel* about what is going on in and around us. They help us check into our hearts, and not just live in our heads. They offer us specific insight and information that we could not see or experience without them.

Our emotions bring high definition to our worlds. Our emotions take us from a fuzzy black and white film of Waikiki Beach to being immersed in every vibrant color, tinkling sound, and intoxicating smell of that tropical paradise. Our emotions are truly our 6th sense, and when we learn to see them that way, we open up a whole new superpower as a woman.

Let's begin with a new way to look at our big feelings.

178

THE BIG BOX OF CRAYONS

Y'all remember back to school supply shopping? Mercy. I loved new school supplies, all of them. But nothing was more exhilarating than a brand-new box of crayons. I can still see their perfectly chiseled tips and smell their waxy goodness now. Although I longed for them every year, my Mom never sprung for the Big Box of 64 crayons. With three kids in school, a mortgage, and plenty of bills to pay, we always got what we needed, but the big box of crayons never made the cut.

Thus my elementary school art masterpieces were limited to the more basic colors, and I learned what it meant to envy your neighbor's possessions. Sixty-four colors *and* a built in crayon sharpener? Come Lord Jesus.

Okay, back to my point here. Think of your emotions like that beautiful, glorious, supersized box of 64 crayons. As High Strung Women our spectrum is bigger and our colors are more vivid. We don't just get red and blue to color our world with- sad or happy, but we get Metallic Gold and Hot Fuchsia - conflicted and elated!

Consider having a conversation with a man about how he is feeling right now. If you can get him to talk, you'll quickly realize that he's only using red and yellow to describe his feelings. Meanwhile, as a woman, we have a full color spectrum with shades of Aqua Blue, Sage Green, Periwinkle Purple, and Buttercup Yellow as we see and express how we feel.

This emotional supersized box of crayons not only gives us more colors to express ourselves, but it also allows us to *see* our world in higher definition, giving us more detail. We have *insight* and *information* that is as specific and powerful as each color, as each emotion. It's a bigger spectrum, and gives us much more detailed insight and articulation as a human being as to what's going on inside of us, as well as discerning the world around us!

Here's an example: by listening to and understanding our emotions, by taking the time to sit and listen without judgement, we can figure out that we're not just "in a bad mood," but that we actually feel frustrated and cramped. We realize that makes us feel angry because we don't like it. That information helps us get to the root of what's really going on: our anger helps us start to search out where we feel our boundaries have been crossed, where we have turned on ourselves, or where we are submitting ourselves to the unrealistic expectation of others.

In taking the time to use our big box of colors- instead of just heading for the bottle of wine, Netflix, and chocolate to numb our bad mood- we have been empowered to see what's really bothering us and what we can do to FIX it.

This EMPOWERS and invigorates us to live our lives and not walk around like a cranky, frustrated victim any longer. That's a major victory in the life of anyone!

ANGER IS YOUR FRIEND

Anger is probably the most widely misunderstood and abused emotion, especially for women. This may sound like a wild thought, but anger is actually a dear, true friend. I love this next section because it shows how closely our boundaries and our emotions work together in the life of a healthy High Strung Woman.

Like most women, I avoided anger like the plague for the majority of my life. We are taught early on that no one likes an angry woman, and then we are pushed off into adulthood with no skills for how to listen to much less honor our anger. I did everything I could not to feel angry, but I have found that anger simply will not be denied.

Anyone who has experienced a breach of their boundaries gets angry, and you know what? We should. Anger serves as the emotional messenger to tell us that something is wrong, that we don't like what is happening. Where we get mad, we need to pay attention. Anger is fiercely honest and will not be shushed.

Anger will shout its truth until we listen to it. But once we listen, it will fade as we work to address what it has shown us. Anger is loud, tenacious, and unreasonable - because it must be. Anger is part of our in-house security system, and you don't want a pushover guarding the gates of your life!

Let's say you are driving on the highway when suddenly someone swerves into your lane, endangering you and everyone around you. Fear surges through your body enabling you to act quickly: you lay on your horn, and slam on your breaks- immediately creating distance between you and the source of the danger. Your physical boundary of safety was breached, and fear and anger sounded the alarm in your personal security system. Fear and anger also unleashed the energy for you to quickly and forcefully re-establish your boundary by getting away from the danger.

Anger is essential to the healthy, full life of a High Strung Woman. It alerts us that something is wrong and gives us the emotional energy we need to push our fence back up, to stand our sacred ground within our boundaries. Anger is a messenger trying to tell us something is wrong, and when we ignore that messenger we are working against ourselves.

Emotions are challenging for any woman, whether she considers herself high-strung or not. We live in a world where emotions are widely misunderstood and neglected, and at the same time, over-indulged and championed as absolute truths. Neither end of that spectrum is healthy.

Emotions are an important part of the equation to find our truth and live at peace with ourselves. They must be honored, but they must also be balanced with the intellect of our minds. When the balance between our emotions and our minds is off, we experience extremes like emotional flooding or total numbing, both of which are terribly hard on us.

But our emotions don't have to be scary or intimidating. We have better options than to only be ruled by our feelings, wildly chaotic and volatile or totally disconnected from them and numb. We are about to learn what to do with all of these big feelings, and if you're willing to lean in, your world is about to get a whole lot brighter! Put on your biggest sunglasses Sis, cause we're about to go ultimate high-def.

QUESTIONS

• How do you respond to emotions you don't like? Do you ignore them?

• Where can you see your emotions still at work inside of you even when you try to ignore them?

• How do you respond to your own anger?

• What beliefs do you have about a woman who expresses anger?

CHAPTER 20

FEELING YOUR FEELINGS

"The only way out is through."

There is an important difference between feeling our feelings and expressing our feelings that must be noted. Although feeling our feelings is what we all seem to fear the most, harm is never done *in the feeling*.

Listen, I get it. Just the thought of letting ourselves feel all of our feelings can make many of us want to curl up into the fetal position and dry heave. But, we *have* to feel our feelings. If we refuse to acknowledge or feel our feelings, we can never learn how to express them in a healthy way, or learn from them! We can't skip this step, but Lord knows I have tried.

We do all kinds of crazy things to avoid feeling our feelings. This panicked aversion to the overwhelming emotions inside of us is the root of so many problems - addictions, work-a-holism, over-eating, under-eating, entire weekends of binging TV, and so much more.

We become a slave to whatever distracts us from feeling.

My personal go-to recipe for numbing and hiding from my feelings is a whole lot of sleep, whirley-pop popcorn covered in butter, loooooads of Diet Coke, hiding in my house and watching an embarrassing amount of Netflix. It's quite the numbing cocktail, but it never helps me deal with what I fear most. Eventually I emerge from my numbed stupor, finding myself rather chubby, lethargic, embarrassed and usually knowing way too much about a British TV series and some new miracle face cream.

Numbing is not a long-term strategy to get happy, find freedom, or overcome anything. Numbing only prolongs our suffering.

One of my greatest fears is that I'll get to the end of my life and find I spent most of my days hiding and numbing instead of bravely facing my demons and showing up as the fierce force of a woman God created me to be. It scares the hell out of me, and still I can hide and numb with the best of them.

I found myself reading *Women, Food, & God* by Geneen Roth in the middle of one of my harshest internal storms. Books are like wise old friends to me, and they always help me find my way home.

Roth teaches powerful truths that help us face our biggest feelings, especially the ones we don't like. She says that *no matter how big they are,* **our feelings cannot destroy us.** *They are just feelings - simply messengers - and they will pass.*

As we have all experienced, ignoring and refusing to feel our feelings just gives them superpowers. They morph into something bigger, scarier and more intimidating than they were ever meant to be.

It is only in allowing our feelings to be whatever they are that we can see and experience that *we are, in fact, bigger than our feelings.* Roth reminds us that we can allow our feelings to rise, grow and even growl without fear. As we ask them to share their story and welcome their message, even if we aren't sure what to do it with yet - they start to fade. We can thank them for their work and watch them flow on down the river. They have done their job.

"I GOT BIG FEELINGS AND I CANNOT LIE..."

Here is a wild truth: our feelings, our emotions cannot lie. They always tell us the truth about what we are really feeling, and in many ways what we really believe.

Our feelings tell us the truth *about what we are feeling*

inside, but they do not always tell us the truth about *what it is really happening outside*.

EXAMPLE: Let's say that while walking up to meet your husband in front of a restaurant you watch a woman walk by, smile and try to flirt with him. Big jealous emotions blow up inside of you. You suddenly feel threatened, insecure and mad. Your feelings are telling you that you don't like what you just saw and that a major boundary was being crossed. The message of your feelings is one of "Danger! Pay attention! This is not okay! Push Back!"

However, after letting your emotions flow before you go storming into making a big scene, you may realize what is really happening is quite innocent. Another woman simply saw what she thought was a single man, and she smiled at him. Your husband smiled back politely and greeted you with a kiss as soon as he saw you. Your feelings react as if you are truly being threatened, and yet these feelings MUST be considered *with* the actual real life facts of what is happening outside of you.

Your emotions told you the truth about *how you felt about what you thought was happening*. But we cannot take how we feel inside as absolute truth about what is actually happening outside of us. Our emotions are a messenger from our subconscious to let us know how we feel about what we think is happening. What we think is happening is based on what we really believe at a subconscious level. Our feelings are supposed to be honored and valued as one part of our discernment in our life.

Here's what I mean in the simplest terms:
- Every time you feel threatened doesn't mean you are actually threatened.
- Every time you feel afraid doesn't mean that you are actually in physical danger.
- Every time you feel lonely doesn't mean that you are truly alone.

If we act only on our feelings every time we have them - we will be chaotic and volatile. (For as you well know, a new feeling comes as steadily as a creek flows.) But if we act solely on our logic and data, we become cold, detached and deeply lonely.

Our magic is in using both our emotional insight and our mind's intelligence to discern our full truth. In addition, listening to our emotions and deep-rooted beliefs give us tremendous insight into how we operate and where we may have internal conflicts.

In the case of our jealousy example, we can discover that we are jealous for our husband's attention and our instinct is to fight for our marriage! We can also realize that our quick jump to big jealousy has highlighted some deep rooted beliefs of insecurity. A wise and emotionally connected woman will recognize this and work to address all of what it means in her life.

Life has a powerful way of showing us what we really believe and what we don't through the revelation of our true feelings. This is where our emotions can be powerful forces of insight. When we learn to listen to our emotions, we can see things we didn't realize were lurking and causing trouble deep within. We don't have to wait until we are in dire circumstances to figure out what's working within us.

QUESTIONS

• Do you avoid your feelings?

• What's your go-to numbing cocktail?

• Are there some feelings you avoid more than others?

• Do you feel like your emotions run you?

• How can you begin to see them as a resource of insight rather than a problem?

CHAPTER 21
HOLD IT ALL IN OR LET IT ALL OUT

**"I've got PMS, OCD and ADD.
I want to cry and look pretty while I kill everyone,
but I can't focus on that right now,
I'm cleaning."**
-Anonymous

This quote makes me feel seen, and although I don't know who said it, I know without a doubt - that girl is a High Strung Woman. Same girl, *same.*

We never have just one or two feelings - we have all of them, ALL AT THE SAME TIME!!!

But What Do We DO With All Of Our Feelings?

Some days it can seem that our lives would go much more smoothly if we just didn't have feelings. But feelings aren't our problem. We just haven't known what the hell to do with them. As a High Strung Woman it can feel like everyone else has a golden retriever in the living room of their hearts, and we're over here with a tiger on a leash like Mike Tyson. What could possibly go wrong?

When we don't know what to do with our fierce, big feelings, we undoubtedly encounter trouble. I know I have. But to be fair, most of us have never been shown how to listen to, honor and befriend our emotions.

We have been told we only have two options when it comes to dealing with our feelings: "let it all out" or "hold it all in."

REPRESSION/"HOLD IT ALL IN"

"I've got a hurricane in my heart, it keeps on rattling the good apart."
-Jillian Jacquelin (Song "God Bless This Mess")

Holding things in has become a way of life for us as women. I mean, hell, we hold in our stomachs, our words and our feelings. We are filled to the brim with truths we have refused to let out. We are living day and night in a pair of emotional super-Spanx, and no one, and I mean no one, should ever have to spend more than three hours in those damn things. Our movements are restricted, our stomachs start to hurt and before long, all we can think about are ripping those suckers off. We become irritable, difficult to deal with and honestly pretty dangerous to those around us.

Am I the only person who thinks that is an awful way to live? And yet, repression is the world's preferred choice when it comes to dealing with emotions.

Most of us learned early on that the world does not like an emotional woman who expresses herself. They disqualify and punish her as irrational and less intelligent. Stinging from the pain of isolation, we push our feelings down, constricting ourselves once again - hoping we can inch closer to some kind of connection.

But our emotions will not be denied. Even if we ignore them in our conscious mind, we know that they continue to operate on a subconscious level. Just like flowing water, our emotions must have somewhere to go. The longer we resist them, the stronger and bigger they become.

EMOTIONS ARE LIKE WATER

The best analogy that I have come across for understanding the nature of our emotions is that of water. Water is the most remarkable substance on Earth. There is no life on our planet without it. Even the smallest amount can make a massive impact. Water can bring a dried, desolate Serengeti back to life, and it can sweep away a city in moments.

Our emotions ebb and flow, they can rage or trickle, but they are always moving and always changing. You can try to force a river where you want it to go, but it will always find a way. Water always finds a way to flow.

The same is true for our emotions. In order for them to be and do all they need to, they must be allowed to FLOW. When they are blocked, we experience a lot of problems.

The physical damage that repressed emotions can do to your health over time is astounding. Mental health professionals have studied the effects of repressed and trapped emotions in the human body. They can grow in intensity, mutate into serious health problems like a disease, or act as an internal wall blocking our energy flow and overall vitality.

Have you found yourself stuck, frustrated or uninspired with your life lately? Not passionate about anything? You have likely blocked the flow of your emotions, and it's cutting you off from yourself. You have to allow them to flow to get your mojo back.

To disconnect a woman from her emotions is to starve her. To connect a woman to her emotions is to bring her back to life.

EXPRESSION/ "LET IT ALL OUT"

Our alternative to repression is expression - "letting it all out." This is the far less socially accepted option, but healthy expression is essential to our emotional health. It requires courage, vulnerability and at the same time, wisdom. There can be great relief in the moment of an unbridled outburst of expression, but there can also be trouble without understanding.

In the heat of the moment, when we express our emotions *to others*, we hand them over to the outside world for affirmation, interpretation and judgement. We take the vulnerable, raw and loaded experience happening inside of us and hand it over to someone else - hoping they will validate us, tell us we're okay and soothe our soul. That can be one hell of a gamble.

With every outburst of expression, what we are really seeking is some kind of emotional *relief*. I mentioned previously that I went the let-it-all-out route earlier in my life because I felt like I was drowning in my feelings. If I didn't express them, I felt like I couldn't breathe.

In this state, we feel like we don't have a choice whether or not to express our feelings. It's like someone shook up a Coke bottle and threw it to the ground bursting open. You feel like you can't stop it, but you also can't undo it after the fact.

This is an important distinction. Expressing our emotions in a healthy way to a trusted friend is *vital* in the healing and growing process as a human. But I believe it's wise to make a big shift from *always expressing* what we feel right when we feel it, to a healthier way of honoring and *working through* our emotions - both for us and those around us.

Brené Brown writes so beautifully about embracing the dare to be vulnerable with our trusted loved ones. We learn to share our feelings to simply *be known* as who and where we are, *not to be agreed with or validated*. It's an intimidating thought at first, but it's a practice that will change your life. I deeply encourage you to start practicing this with some of your most trusted friends. You don't need to share everything - every feeling, thought or judgement. But take some time, identify what is important and share so someone else knows where you are. And then, my dear sister, dare to LISTEN. We can let everyone be exactly where they are. Don't give advice or try to fix: just sit with them and let them sit with you in your honesty.

That kind of interaction will change everything you know about real connection and intimacy. I guarantee it. It is brave, free and deeply connected in a way you've never known. You don't have to be the same, or in the same emotional place to be connected. You can simply connect in knowing and being known right where you are.

UNHEALTHY EXPRESSIONS

No matter how intense, big or fast our emotions are, *we* are responsible for how we express our feelings. When we take out how we are feeling on someone or something else, we are on dangerous ground. It's unfair, scary and harmful to our targets, and can be absolutely abusive. I know that's some strong language, but if you've ever been on the receiving end, you know it's true. We are here to learn how to stop the cycle of hurt and find healing.

Let's start with identifying some unhealthy ways of expressing our feelings.

- Physical violence of any kind is unacceptable as a means of expressing your emotions - to yourself, to others or to animals. Unless you are fighting to escape a physical attack (which should never happen a second time), violence is never your answer.
- Yelling, screaming or berating others around you for any reason is not acceptable. We all get into disagreements or heated arguments from time to time (especially if you are married... bless). But screaming at someone is not okay. I'm a yeller when I get panicked that someone is refusing to listen to me, so I can struggle here. But screaming does not help anything. It only escalates the situation. We can find better means of expressing how we feel. If you find yourself screaming, walk away. Take a walk, do a workout, take a nap. Come back when you can talk calmly and clearly.
- Relentlessly talking to, crying to and hanging onto someone is not okay. As we have discussed with

boundaries, there are limits for all of us. We need to be aware of when we are crossing the line and where we are trying to use someone as an emotional sedative. If you find yourself realizing that you can talk and talk about the same problem and have no idea that an hour has flown by, here is a tip: set a timer on your phone for five minutes. Allow yourself to share your feelings with your loved one freely for those five minutes, and when the timer goes off, stop. Take a deep breath, and redirect the conversation to *them*. Ask them what they have going on and what they are excited about. You'll be amazed how much better you feel talking about someone other than yourself! If you find that you simply cannot stop talking about the issue- seek help from a therapist or counselor right away. (I've been there- trust me.)

When we engage in any of these behaviors others have every right to distance themselves or limit our access to them. We must learn from the natural consequences of our own actions, even when we are in emotional distress.

HEALTHY EXPRESSIONS:

Finding a healthy way for us to express our feelings is of the utmost importance. Learning the best ways to welcome and express our feelings is how we move from fearing our feelings to befriending them. There are many ways that allow our emotions to flow out of us that honor the emotion, ourselves and others. In fact, the right expression for you may just unlock a new talent, hobby or creative outlet that does much more for your life than just serve as an outlet for your feelings. I personally love a combination of several activities, but let's see what resonates with you.

PHYSICAL ACTIVITY

This is a place that we can begin to see how powerful our emotions are as a source of energy, 'cause girl, you 'bout to turn into the *Hulk*.

- Running, working out, resistance training, lifting weights and getting your heart rate up, in some way or another, is a great way to express your feelings.
- My sister goes on interval runs when she needs to work out her feelings, my girl Allison goes to shoot skeet in a field, my mom scrubs her house, demos bathrooms and does manual labor like landscaping or moving furniture. Getting really sweaty and red-faced seems to be important for working out our big, fast emotions.
- "Non-burst," physical activities like yoga, a long walk, painting or singing or playing your heart out an instrument are also very powerful tools.

It's amazing how quickly we find clarity, sometimes even in the middle of these activities. Expressing our emotions in a healthy way allows them to flow, which enables us to freely process and address their message.

EMOTIONAL/MENTAL ACTIVITY

The quieter way of expressing your emotions is through internal expression. I found this incredibly helpful in seasons when I felt I didn't have healthy enough relationships to express my emotions in a safe space. We all express ourselves differently, and as a creative, this is one of my go-to processes.

- I am a journaling fool, Sis. I love to journal, especially after I got over being afraid that one day my future children would find my journal and cringe at the horrors of my honesty. Pouring my heart out on page after page helps me fully connect to what I am feeling, ask questions and express without fear. It's not always pretty, but it's always honest.

- Journaling is a way to verbally vomit without actually vomiting on anyone. And if you find that you round a corner and don't feel that way anymore, you just can rip that page out and burn it. In addition, there's something bold and audacious when you put pen to paper and let 'er rip. We need to let our emotions flow, and we only get to the other side when we let them flow unrestricted in a healthy way.

I am not saying you go all *Mean Girls* and make a "burn book," but journaling is a great way to check in with yourself honestly and keep track of how you're feeling. If at the end of a month you look back and you're like, "Wow, I have felt angry every day this month and didn't even realize it!" You can use that as a clue that you need to really address your feelings, talk to a therapist or find an actual solution to your frustrations.

- Write a letter to whoever you are upset with in radical honesty. Let it sit. Come back to it and read it again if you need to. Without ever delivering your letter you may find this a powerfully effective expression. You can burn it, shred it or keep it. You'll know what to do.
- Use the energy of your emotions to *create* in expression: write, make music, paint, dance, design, plant, sculpt, build. I love the magic of creating out of deep emotions. I guarantee some of your favorite songs, works of art or books were created in the fires of emotional expression.
- Sometimes our emotions are complex and deep, and so using a tool like meditation can really help us dig out what's really going on, and allow us to process them in thought and breath. Use whatever works best for you. The best way is whatever way *you* find most helpful.

- If you find yourself stuck in an emotion, in a pattern or in despair - get yourself to a therapist or counselor. Life is far too short to live stuck in one emotion or pattern. There is an incredible network of help and emotional support available to anyone who seeks it.

During these expressions we can realize things like:
"I didn't see it before, but now I realize I've been feeling like I had to work to get this new girl in our group to like me. The pressure to prove myself worthy made me irritated because I didn't like it. Now I realize that I don't have to get her to like me. I like me, and that is enough. But my emotion of anger/frustration's message was to tell me that I was trying to do something I didn't want to do (breaking my boundary), and that it didn't feel right. I'm grateful for this message-because it brought me back to my truth, back to myself."

When we express our emotions in healthy ways, we experience powerful breakthroughs.

QUESTIONS:

- Do your feelings often feel bigger than you? Do you feel like they swallow you up?

- Do you allow your emotions to flow freely?

• What emotions do you now allow to flow freely? Which ones do you avoid at all costs?

• Have you experienced pain, hurt, or abuse at the hands of someone else's "expressions?"

• Do you have any unhealthy ways of expressing your feelings?

• What new way of expression can you try to both honor your feelings and take responsibility for how you treat others in your feelings?

CHAPTER 22
FOR BEST RESULTS: PROCESS

We've learned about the dangers of repressing our feelings, and the need for healthy emotional expression. But there is a step beyond healthy expression, where we learn to *process* our feelings. We work with our emotions to work through them and learn from them. There is no way around our feelings: the only way out is through our feelings.

Since we no longer have to fear our emotions, we throw open the door to allow ourselves to feel all of what we are feeling. We let them rise in intensity and strength. We express our emotions in a healthy way if we need to, and then we listen to their message. We can then thank them, and release them to flow on down the river.

Here's an example. You learn from someone that a friend has betrayed and embarrassed you. They have flat out done you wrong and everyone knows it.

As you sting with shock, denial tries to take over. But as you breathe and welcome your emotions, a hot wave of anger starts to rise inside of you. As you allow the anger and let it rise, you may feel rejected, perhaps embarrassed that you didn't see this coming. As you process your anger and shame (whether in moments or days) your feelings may eventually flow from anger to hurt, to pain. The sting of shame may lessen over time as you realize you didn't deserve this, but the painful ache of experiencing this kind of betrayal can throb. As you process your sadness and your hurt, you may then feel grief. Grief for the loss of trust, the loss of innocence in your friendship. As you allow and process your grief, you find the energy and resolve to distance yourself from this untrustworthy person. As time passes and you get some distance, you may then even find yourself feeling pity, or compassion for this person who made such a poor decision. You feel the heaviness this offense has brought on your heart and decide it is time to release it. You are able to choose to let them go, bless them and walk on as a wiser, more experienced woman. You have honored yourself, your emotions, and because you did not refuse or get stuck in any part of the process, you are then able to freely release and move on.

What.a.ride.

And yet, all of those feelings are important at every single stage of processing. We can get stuck refusing to allow the feelings we don't like. For some of us it's anger. For some of us it's sadness or grief if we think they are weak. For others it's the pain of dealing with rejection. But we have to allow all of them, embrace them and let them flow. Our feelings provide the insight and the energy to *do* the things we need to do like distance ourselves from a hurtful, untrustworthy person and not be held captive in offense.

Denying our emotions at any point in this process will prohibit us from what we long for - finding peace and freedom from the offense. We find freedom from offense in forgiveness, but we don't get there any other way than through the road of our fiercely honest emotions.

Real forgiveness cannot be faked, and to get there, we cannot deny even our most outrageous feelings.

Allowing our feelings to flow isn't a magic pill. It doesn't mean once we let them flow they won't ever come back. But you'll get to a place of peace a hell of a lot quicker when you let them flow back and forth, and back again. It's messy but essential in the life of any High Strung Woman.

We must forever abandon this belief that our feelings and emotions are bad, uncontrollable forces that must be caged up, like Pandora's Box. That is a lie designed by the enemy to bottle us up, hold us back and take us out of the arena of life.

Our feelings serve a powerful purpose in connecting us to our subconscious, which is ruled by our beliefs. Our emotions connect us to the truth of how we really feel, and what we really believe. If there is a major disconnect between what you "think" you believe and what you feel, your feelings don't lie about what you really believe. There are some incredible coaches and therapists who can work with you to align these two forces and free you of the internal conflict keeping you from progress and success in key areas of your life.

Do you want to live an enlightened, exceptional, powerful life as a strong woman? Then Sis, we've got to make friends with our emotions. Better yet, we need to make her our best friend forever. We will be amazed at her insight and command.

I need you to know that these chapters are NOT written from a place of expertise - far from it. I have not arrived, especially emotionally, and I will spend the rest of my life reading these pages back to my soul to remind me of what I believe and what I am aiming for. Many of us try to box up our emotions and never face them because they are complicated, messy and never "done." But I suppose that is why we are to live day by glorious day. Because without our emotions, we aren't really living.

QUESTIONS:

• How can you begin to welcome your emotions?

• Think of a situation where you refused to allow your emotions and they came out anyway. How could processing your emotions helped you get to a place of peace and resolution sooner? Take some time to write out what that could have looked like?

CHAPTER 23
FLASH FLOODS

Some of my most challenging experiences as a High Strung Woman have been the times when my emotions came in so strong and fast, that they swept me off of my feet. It was as if I was hit by a flash flood - a rushing flood of emotions that I didn't see coming, and before I knew it, I was fighting the crashing waves to breathe. These aren't regular emotional experiences - they don't happen every day - but I believe they are often a hallmark in the life of a High Strung Woman.

Meteorologists consider flash floods to be incredibly dangerous because they combine the force of massive flood waters with incredible speed. They occur when the ground cannot absorb any more rainfall, and as we know, water *has* to go somewhere. It has to flow.

In South Texas, where our limestone hills and sandy clay soil don't absorb much moisture, flooding can come in a deadly flash under a sunny sky. Water collects rapidly miles and miles upstream, and can come crashing down a dry riverbed, rising up to 30 to 40 feet in minutes.

The greatest danger is that you can have no idea it's coming.

Have you ever gone about your day thinking you were fine, only to be taken out by a flash flood of emotions in the shampoo aisle at Target?

Have you ever found yourself crashed over by wave upon wave of emotion? Struggling to know up from down, not able to catch your breath, and feeling like you have no choice but to try and cry, yell, or fight them out?

It can feel like there's no stopping it when those flood waters break loose.

My worst emotional flash floods usually involved heartbreak. Heartbreak has a way of flooding our emotions and refusing to be reasonable. When we feel abandoned, lonely or betrayed, many of us don't know what else to do other than rush to express our emotions to whoever will listen. As wave upon wave crashes over us, we will be swept down river and lose ourselves if we don't find an anchor.

Panicked to find something to hold onto, we often grab onto other people. Although we need to be able to express our feelings in a safe space, if we are looking to them to save us, we are holding on too tight. By relentlessly crying to them, talking about our heartache, and relying on them to hold us up we end up dragging them into our flash flood. This can go on for hours, days, even years in some cases. Once we "wake up," we can find ourselves miles and miles downstream, not even sure how we go there or what damage has been done along the way.

I've experienced it in some places almost as a *blackout*. I was so angry, so hurt, so afraid that I just sort of emotionally "raged." I was carried swiftly downriver by the powerful current of my emotional flood. We can rage in fear, we can rage in grief, we can rage in anger.

It's not pretty.

It's usually downright ugly. Not because we should feel shame in having our emotions, but often in trying to survive the flood of our feelings, we tend to hurt ourselves, others and even innocent bystanders along the way.

In the middle of the swell, you can feel as if you have no choice. It just comes crashing inside of you and out of you, wave upon wave, until the waves carry you with them. You wash up miles down the river beaten up, empty and often ashamed.

Are we supposed to spend our lives as High Strung Women being swept up in the torrent downstream of our emotions, and then stumbling our way back to a healthy place?

NO.

Even when the flash floods come, we do not have to fear our big, strong emotions. But we do desperately need anchors in our lives. TRUTHS that are bigger than our feelings, no matter how big they grow. Truths we can hold onto when the flash floods come, and truths that will remain long after the flood waters have receded.

AN ANCHOR FOR YOUR SOUL

As we have learned, boundaries are essential for us as High Strung Women. They help us identify our sacred ground, our sweet spot, and they protect us. Boundaries also act as anchors when the floodwaters of our emotions rise.

This is **_vital_** for every High Strung Woman. We MUST have anchor points of truth in our lives that are bigger and stronger than our changing emotions, and we must hold them as sacred. Truth does not change no matter how we are feeling. Truth is bigger than everything else.

I can remember a time in college when I was drowning emotionally. I mean it - I was a wreck. I was drowning in heartache, rejection and the sting of a breakup. My feelings were telling me this relationship was everything I ever wanted and I wanted to believe that it's what God had for me. And yet, the guy had _broken up with me_. My fiercely strong emotions were in direct contradiction with my reality.

Shaking in that storm, thrashing in the waters of my emotional flash flood, I remember asking my Dad how on earth you're supposed to know, like really know, what God was saying to you. How could you know what was His voice and what wasn't?

He listened with the compassion of a father who hated seeing his daughter in pain. He knew all too well the stormy sea of my mind and emotions. He then said, "Ab, our emotions, our feelings change, they will always change, but the Word of God never will. God never changes."

He asked me what God had been speaking to me, what verses had been on my heart and encouraged me to CLING to them with all I had. He promised me that they would only be proven to be even more true, and they would provide a shelter from my storm.

This is a lifeline for us as High Strung Women. We have intense, powerful feelings that can sweep us away but an anchor helps us stay in and stand our sacred ground, no matter what our feelings are doing. We are able to cling to the anchor of truth and no matter how the flood swells, we aren't consumed in it.

This is where we remember that our emotions are only part of our equation in discerning real truth. We use our minds to cling to the anchors of unshakeable facts, of truth, and consider them with the message of our emotions.

Beyond just Scriptures, we need to develop our own personal anchors of truth. Write them out, share them with our people and remind ourselves of them often.

Some of my own anchors include:
- Jesus is BIGGER than anything I face, anything I am feeling. HE IS ALWAYS BIGGER. This settles me profoundly and ignites my faith all at the same time.
- My priorities and responsibilities include following Jesus, honoring my true self, choosing to honor my husband and my marriage, and loving well.
- I am a freedom fighter: I want freedom in my soul more than anything else, thus friction in my life is expected: not always a sign that something is wrong.
- God gave me a rebel heart to rebel against places of bondage, and seek out and share how He brings FREEDOM to our hearts like a proven warrior.
- I am worthy, loved and created to do incredible things. I am not normal. I was made to stand out, to be full on

100-proof ME.

- No one's opinion, interpretation of, or expectation on my life matters except for the Lord's, and mine.
- I can trust God to handle my reputation and deal with those who don't understand me. They'll work it out. We'll both be fine.
- People can be crazy, selfish and self-serving. They'll never totally see it your way. You can't win everyone over. It's impossible, so I'm going to love my people hard and leave the rest to God.
- I am not a victim. Any place I allow myself to be one, I will be miserable, because I am wrong.
- God made all of me. All of who I am, how I am wired and what burns inside of me, ON PURPOSE, and what He made is GOOD.
- I value bravery over perfection. Showing up is more important and more valuable than showing off every damn time.
- No one is inspired, or empowered by perfection. Courage, even messy courage, is contagious.
- I am worthy of a life that I love.
- I am 100-percent responsible for my life. Everyone else is responsible for their own. That is EMPOWERING.
- God will work all things together FOR MY GOOD. No one can mess that up.

These truths are incredibly important when my feelings are telling me that God can't possibly love me - that I am not good enough, I am alone or that I should be ashamed of failing yet again.

My feelings are insights to what I truly believe, and my God is in the business of healing us from the inside out. He binds the wounds and the broken places of our lives to His truth, and He heals us. He heals and changes what we believe, even about ourselves. Like a broken bone needs a cast to heal properly, God's truths heal us and make us stronger.

I believe with all of my heart that where you find real truth, about anything, you cannot help but run smack dab into JESUS. That's why helping women find their truths, finding freedom, and coming into their own gets me so fired up. THAT is where Jesus met me.

God met me on the hot, scorched dirt of the arena of my life - in the truths of who I really was, not who I was "supposed" to be. He welcomed the intense, sassy, strong willed, feisty little rebel heart that I am. The one that did not fit in anywhere.

Jesus meets us all on the holy ground of who we really are, where we really are and how we really are. It is our true selves that must choose Him, not the manufactured, "best version" of ourselves. He is not a God of appearances. He is a God of reality.

So Sis, throw wide the doors to your real self and invite Him in. Watch in wonder as He heals, makes new and brings FIRE to all of who you really are. He has a knack for it, because as we so easily forget, He designed you and sent you to this world to shake things up just by being YOU.

Why would the God who made you want you to be anything other than who He made you to be? The REAL YOU???

If you aren't sure how to "throw wide the doors to your heart" to this God, this Jesus that I keep saying is crazy about you, and is just waiting to show up in your life, it's incredibly simple. Praying is just talking to God- it gets easier the more you do it, just like getting to know a friend and talk with them.

What better friend could we ask for than the reigning King Of The Universe? So if you need a little help, feel free to whisper this prayer....

"God, I almost can't believe it, but I hear that You actually aren't mad at me, that You long to be my best friend, my heavenly Father. To advocate for me, protect me, to love me

and lead me into the incredible life You have for me. I don't even know that I really understand all of that, but what I do know is that my heart is open. I know that I am imperfect, I mess up all the time and that You are not just perfect, but You are holy! So I open my heart and my hands and I receive what Your Son Jesus did on the cross for me, to wash away, to forgive everything I have done wrong and everything I ever will do wrong. You made a way for me to come into incredible relationship with You. I can't earn it and I can't ruin it. There is now no reason for me to ever hesitate to come to You, I am Your beloved, most cherished daughter. I am fiercely loved. Jesus- you have saved me, and now I ask for You to fill me. In Jesus Name, Amen."

God loves you and He is WILD about you. Welcome to the fam Sis. Your adventure is only beginning. He is so, so good.

As much grief as I gave the Southern Baptists, these saints know a thing or two about clinging to anchors of TRUTH in the face of all kinds of hell. Growing up in that church house, you learned and sang a lot of hymns straight out of that hymnal. Hymns are generational old songs, not written in search of a worship "experience" (can we get some more of that up in here please), but lyrics penned and melodies raised to stir the faith, the souls of God's children by declaring His unshakeable truths.

I love the old hymn, "He Hideth My Soul," and find myself singing it *to* myself a lot of days. When I think about the storms of life, whether they be outside of me or inside of me, what a picture it is to be hidden in a small cleft, a cave just my size, in the side of a MOUNTAIN of ROCK.

There is no safer place to be, no haven more secure than hidden in the rock of God's TRUTHS and covered there with His Hand.

"He hideth my soul in the cleft of the rock
That shadows a dry, thirsty land
He hideth my life in the depths of His love
And covers me there with His hand
And covers me there with His hand"
- Fanny Crosby

QUESTIONS

• What are your flash flood triggers?

• What are some of your anchor points?

• Begin to work on your list of unshakeable truths.

CHAPTER 24
THE WORLD NEEDS YOU.
YOUR WORLD NEEDS YOU.

My brave sister, we've spent much time in these pages learning how to show up for ourselves, care for ourselves and choose ourselves, because the world desperately needs the real you. *Your world* desperately needs the real you. Your family, your kids, your friends, your peers, your community, your generation, your country needs the real, full on, 100-proof YOU.

It's a daily process to learn how to live out of who we really are. And hell yeah Sis: it's gonna be messy. You'll have moments of glory when you are uninhibited, brave and fully alive. You will also likely follow that up at some point with an experience where you find yourself feeling small, rejected and striving.

But here is what I can tell you: daring to show up as the real you in every moment of every day, is the fight of your life. And it should be.

If we go through life as anything other than who we really are, we are not really living. It's not us out in the arena. It's our substitute, and nothing is ever as good as the real thing. Is your understudy getting her ass kicked out there? It's time for you to put the imposter on the bench and get in there yourself Sis.

Only the real you can win your battles.

We also cannot find true connection in the world or in our relationships when we are anything, and I mean ANYTHING other than who we really are. Everything else is built on pretense. It's a faulty foundation, and it's only a matter of time before it tumbles. Don't spend your life trying to quick fix a faulty foundation. Don't settle for a fixer upper relationship, Sis. Wait it out, wait for the beautiful house with the solid foundation. You bring your best and trust God to bring His.

Getting honest and going full on YOU will immediately tick some people off, but it will also bind your heart to others. It becomes easier when we learn not to hold on so tight. Open your hands, trust your heavenly Father, and at all costs, follow Jesus. Listen to what burns in your soul, honor what feels right and respect what feels wrong.

Writing this book has been one of the greatest challenges and most intimidating places of vulnerability of my life. But another one of my anchors of truth is that courage is contagious. So this is me choosing courage over perfection, daring to be seen in my messy expression of all of who I am, and praying and believing that perhaps, just perhaps, the true story of a wild-eyed preacher's daughter who dared to be herself just might make you a little more brave, too.

You are a fierce, beautiful creature as a High Strung Woman, and I am honored to call you my sister. You'll never know what it means to me to realize I am not the only High Strung Woman trying to find her way in this world.

I'll leave you with this. We are big fans of Theodore Roosevelt in this house. Ryan has had something of an obsession with the renegade president who rattled his generation. One of our favorite quotes is the "Man In The Arena" speech T.R. gave in Paris in 1910. I became much more familiar with it after reading "Daring Greatly," by Brené Brown, and in my opinion, it is as close to gospel as I think you can get without being an apostle.

As I wrestled with how to end this book, I came back to Roosevelt's charge to live our lives in the arena. I knew I had to use his words to send you off, but just with my own little spin on it. Because, well, you know by now - I'm always going to do it my own way!

This is for you my High Strung Sisters. I adore you. I am so honored to call you my friends.

"IT IS NEVER THE CRITIC WHO COUNTS; NOT THE WOMAN WHO POINTS OUT HOW THE OTHER WOMAN STUMBLES, OR WHERE SHE COULD HAVE DONE BETTER,

NO, THE CREDIT BELONGS TO THE FIERCE WOMAN WHOSE FEET ARE PLANTED IN THE ARENA OF HER OWN LIFE, WHOSE FACE IS MARRED BY THE DUST AND SWEAT AND BLOOD THAT COMES FROM DARING TO REFUSE TO BE ANYONE OTHER THAN WHO SHE REALLY IS;

SHE ERRS, SHE COMES UP SHORT AGAIN AND AGAIN, BUT SHE ALWAYS CHOOSES TO RISE FROM THE DIRT- BECAUSE SHE KNOWS- THERE IS NO EFFORT WITHOUT ERROR AND SHORTCOMING;

SHE KNOWS THAT TO FIGHT, FALL, RISE AND LIVE STANDING ON THE ARENA DIRT IS THE ONLY WAY TO TRULY LIVE.

SHE IS NOT A SPECTATOR, POINTING OUT WHERE OTHERS COULD DO BETTER. EVERY DAY SHE STRIVES TO BE REAL, BRAVE, KIND AND TO DO IT ALL HER OWN WAY.

SHE KNOWS THE GLORY OF A LIFE LIVED AND CELEBRATED AS WHO SHE REALLY IS, AND AT THE SAME TIME, SHE KNOWS THE PAIN OF REJECTION BY THOSE DEAR SOULS THAT SIMPLY AREN'T BRAVE ENOUGH YET. SHE IS DANGEROUS TO A WORLD OF CLIQUES, SYSTEMS AND PROGRAMS - BECAUSE NO MATTER HOW

HER WORLD RESPONDS TO HER, SHE CANNOT BE
BOUGHT.

SHE IS A FIERCE FORCE OF A WOMAN WHO KNOWS THE
INCOMPARABLE VALUE OF WHO SHE IS, AND HER
GREATEST AIM IS TO SHOW UP AS HER TRUE SELF IN
EVERY PLACE THAT LIFE TAKES HER.
IN BEING FULLY AND UNAPOLOGETICALLY HERSELF,
SHE WILL CHANGE HER WORLD."

Adapted From Theodore Roosevelt's
"The Man In The Arena"
April 23, 1910

CONNECT WITH ABBI

INSTAGRAM:
@abbiwalkerofficial and @highstrungwoman
#highstrungwoman #COAHSW
#proudtobeahighstrungwoman #abbiwalker

FACEBOOK:
Confessions Of A High Strung Woman
Abbi Walker Official

WEBSITE:
www.abbiwalker.net
www.abbiwalkermusic.com

MUSIC:
You can find Abbi's albums Feisty, Kiss Kiss Bang Bang, and
Hope Of A Little Green on iTunes, Spotify, and Amazon
Music.

PODCAST:
The "Confessions Of A High Strung Woman" podcast can be
found anywhere podcasts are available, as well as on the
website.

THE HIGH STRUNG WOMAN'S CREED

"IT IS NEVER THE CRITIC WHO COUNTS; NOT THE WOMAN WHO POINTS OUT HOW THE OTHER WOMAN STUMBLES, OR WHERE SHE COULD HAVE DONE BETTER.

NO, THE CREDIT BELONGS TO THE FIERCE WOMAN WHOSE FEET ARE PLANTED IN THE ARENA OF HER OWN LIFE, WHOSE FACE IS MARRED BY THE DUST AND SWEAT AND BLOOD THAT COMES FROM DARING TO REFUSE TO BE ANYONE OTHER THAN WHO SHE REALLY IS;

SHE ERRS, SHE COMES UP SHORT AGAIN AND AGAIN, BUT SHE ALWAYS CHOOSES TO RISE FROM THE DIRT- BECAUSE SHE KNOWS- THERE IS NO EFFORT WITHOUT ERROR AND SHORTCOMING;

SHE KNOWS THAT TO FIGHT, FALL, RISE AND LIVE STANDING ON THE ARENA DIRT IS THE ONLY WAY TO TRULY LIVE.

SHE IS NOT A SPECTATOR, POINTING OUT WHERE OTHERS COULD DO BETTER. EVERY DAY SHE STRIVES TO BE REAL, BRAVE, KIND AND TO DO IT ALL HER OWN WAY.

SHE KNOWS THE GLORY OF A LIFE LIVED AND CELEBRATED AS WHO SHE REALLY IS, AND AT THE SAME TIME, SHE KNOWS THE PAIN OF REJECTION BY THOSE DEAR SOULS THAT SIMPLY AREN'T BRAVE ENOUGH YET.

SHE IS DANGEROUS TO A WORLD OF CLIQUES, SYSTEMS AND PROGRAMS - BECAUSE NO MATTER HOW HER WORLD RESPONDS TO HER, SHE CANNOT BE BOUGHT.

SHE IS A FIERCE FORCE OF A WOMAN WHO KNOWS THE INCOMPARABLE VALUE OF WHO SHE IS, AND HER GREATEST AIM IS TO SHOW UP AS HER TRUE SELF IN EVERY PLACE THAT LIFE TAKES HER.

IN BEING FULLY AND UNAPOLOGETICALLY HERSELF, SHE WILL CHANGE HER WORLD.

RESOURCES

BOOKS

Boundaries: When to Say Yes, How to Say No to Take Control of Your Life
by Dr. Henry Cloud and Dr. John Townsend

Women, Food, And God : An Unexpected Path To Almost Everything
and
This Messy Magnificent Life: A Field Guide To Mind, Body, and Soul
by Geneen Roth

Daring Greatly: How the Courage to Be Vulnerable Transforms the Way We Live, Love, Parent, and Lead
by Brenè Brown

The Language Of Letting Go: Daily Meditations For Codependents
by Melody Beattie

MEDITATIONS
Breathe App
Calm App
(Available through app store)

Made in the USA
Columbia, SC
05 March 2021